B
Mega

MEGA WEIRD

STORIES FROM THE ANXIETY-RIDDEN MIND OF NICHOLAS MEGALIS

ARTIST.
MUSICIAN.
IDIOT.

MEGA WEIRD

NICHOLAS MEMPHIS

THANK YOU to my mom, my dad, my sister, and my brother. I'm so, so sorry. Also thank you to BBG, my friends, and everyone who has ever believed in me or at least lied and said they did. I LOVE YOU MORE THAN PIZZA.

Regan Arts.
65 Bleecker Street
New York, NY 10012

Names and identifying details of some of the people portrayed in this book have been changed.

First Regan Arts paperback edition March 2015.
Library of Congress Control Number: 2014955530
ISBN 978-1-941393-61-1
Cover design by Richard Ljoenes
Interior paintings and illustrations by Tom Megalis
Book design by Jacob Covey | Unflown
Printed in China
10 9 8 7 6 5 4 3 2 1

CONTENTS

YOUR TRIBE IS YOUR TRIBE

I don't know what I am. And I don't really care.

I've spent my entire life trying to figure it out, and it's pretty much driven me nuts. We waste so much time on this rock in the sky searching for the truth like it actually *exists*. The only truth is that if you're reading this, you're still alive. And if you're still alive, you've won the lottery, because so many people are *dead*. So dance your ass off. Seriously, right now, shake your ass.

I owe it to my parents for laying the bricks for me to build my little world. In said world, I am happy. My scrawny arms are toned, my unibrow is trimmed, and my weirdness is currency. You don't need to struggle to exist in someone else's dream. You can construct your own dream and surround yourself with the magic that keeps you alive.

We are all just flies in a swimming pool. We have no control. People like me pretend we have control so that we don't lose our minds on transatlantic flights. Oh, and I have not really matured. Nope. I am still sneaking cigarettes and junk food. I love naked women and playing the guitar. And if there were more trees in New York City, I would probably have a tree house by now.

They will call you "different," they will call you "weird," and hallelujah! Take it as a sign that you are doing something right. Your tribe is your tribe; your brain is your brain. Fucked up or not. Be loud, be stupid, and if you're going to fail, fail beautifully. When you wake up in the morning, tie your shoes or don't. I never learned how. And that's perfectly okay.

From the anxiety capital of the world,
with love in my heart
and pizza in my stomach,
NICHOLAS MEGALIS

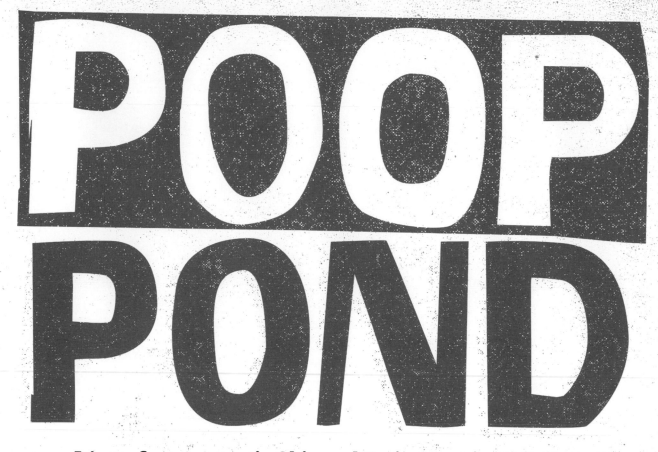

POOP POND

It's my first summer in Ohio, and I'm just turning thirteen.

I have zero friends. Well, I have one friend if you include my journal—the 99-cent spiral notebook where I draw titties incessantly and conduct imaginary *Rolling Stone* interviews with myself. The book is littered with egomaniacal questions like "Mr. Megalis, how does it feel to have four albums under your belt?" and "Mr. Megalis, you're widely considered to be a legend and a genius. Does this play into your writing process?"

I'm just starting to settle into a new school district in a quiet, superwhite neighborhood in the suburbs of Cleveland. (If you ever need to find a white person, you can come to my neighborhood. We have plenty.) Tiny 73-year-old Mrs. Daltree stands on the corner with a huge mallet, hammering a homemade sign into the lawn with THE DEVIL IS REAL scrawled in crooked, blood-drip letters. I don't think she realizes how fucking awesome it looks. She douses her petunias with nasty, pungent coyote piss to keep deer from eating them. Her yard smells like Grand Central Station's lower-level men's room after rush hour.

It's a blistering-hot Monday afternoon on the back porch of my suburban Fortress of Solitude. I protect my soft, hairless skin with globs of sunblock (as generously applied by my fearful mother). "Nick, you don't want fucking cancer!" she warns in her typically expletive-laced momspeak. I'm lathered head to toe in the cancer-stopping goo and ready for my 2:30 p.m. pickup. I've just made my first friend. Glory be to God! His name is Brian. Brian and I met in the library parking lot a week earlier. He was riding his bike, and I was riding mine, and our gigantic, dorky retard helmets were both the same tint of blue. *Boom!* Bond formed. Now Brian and his dad are on their way to pick me up for a day of "fun" at their house. And just like all the plans I make, I'm already regretting it deeply.

By the time Brian and his daddy driver, Mr. Bazalski, arrive, my stomach is a total wreck. The anxiety of this blossoming friendship has gotten the best of me. In retrospect, I should have just canceled my plans, cleared my bowels, and watched a movie with my dog. But I am petrified of blowing it with the only kid I know, and I don't want to waste the $3,000 worth of sunscreen that my mom just poured on me. As Brian's dad pulls his shitty 1999 Toyota Camry into our driveway that my own dad was too Greek to have repaved, I can feel the shitstorm brewing. And I'm being as literal as I can here. . . .

"Hey, Mr. Nick!" Brian's dad greets me in a way-too-happy tone. Why is he so goddamn ecstatic? Did he win money this morning? Did he do a bump of coke before he left the house? His glee appalls me. I briefly glance over at Brian, who has made room for me in the backseat. Brian is a big boy, and he always has snacks on him. None of which he ever shares with me. On the measly fifteen-minute car trip, Brian annihilates a fanny pack filled with fruit chews and a canteen of diet root beer like some diabetic Boy Scout. Brian and I are both socially stunted, so we barely say a word to each other on the ride to the Bazalski house. Brian chuckles under his breath when I ask if they have a bathroom I can use. He has no idea how deadly serious I am.

When we arrive at Brian's, and as I get up to leave the backseat, I notice something more horrible than anything I have ever seen. Right there, the size of a dime, is a shit spot. My bowels have leaked. I am beyond mortified. My heart is about to explode. I want to escape, but I can't move my muscles. Brian *cannot* see this. I have to do something. I spot a newspaper on the floor of the backseat and toss it onto the poop. I imagine that it has probably smeared it around more, but I don't want to look.

I'm afraid I might wake the shit-beast inside of me.

I slam the car door and head toward the house with my new friend and his overly excited father. My butt cheeks are clenched together so tightly that I can barely walk. I hop, actually, like a penguin about to have explosive diarrhea.

The house is immaculate. It smells fantastic. I'm actually angry at how beautiful and clean this house is. Brian's mom is busy in their glorious, sprawling kitchen. She turns to greet me with a raised oven mitt and a smile as wide as Ohio. *"Hey, Mr. Nick!"* she laugh-talks. So excited to meet me. Or pretend-excited. I can't tell. The scent of mashed potatoes and gravy wafts through the house, covering up the scent of my volcanic ass. I can't walk over to the kitchen because I'm afraid I might wake the shit-beast inside of me. I wave at her from afar—far enough so that she can't see me profusely sweating from having to shit so badly.

My eyes dart around like a Navy Seal, scoping out the nearest facilities. I'm in full panic mode. Any moment now, my shorts will be three times their weight. Brian is still beside me, and I can't imagine that he doesn't smell the horrid farts that are escaping. I am filling up the foyer with nauseating fumes, and I can't wait any longer. "Brian, where's your bathroom?" I frantically whisper. Brian points to a door along the hallway, not saying a word. Somehow I am able to hold the poop in long enough to enter the bathroom and close the door, but not long enough to make it to the bowl. My butt explodes, remodeling their bathroom walls and floor to resemble a Jackson Pollock painting. If I said I was in full panic mode before, consider this

CODE BROWN: PANIC OVER-LOAD.

This is my nightmare. Brian and his Norman Rockwell–looking family are out there preparing a meal for me, and I'm on my hands and knees scrubbing my own excrement from their new tile floor. I am naked from the waist down, crying and sweating profusely. I stand up to flush the wads of toilet paper, and I catch a glimpse of my beet-red face in the mirror. I look like a psycho. Like I just murdered someone. I examine my shorts. Miraculously, they're clean. It's my underwear that is absolutely destroyed, with no hope of recovery. I pull up my shorts and wrap the mutilated underwear in toilet paper. I hold the only evidence that remains in my hands.

I crack the bathroom door and peer out. The Bazalskis are nowhere to be found. Thank you, Jesus. The coast is clear, but I have to dispose of this mess as quickly as possible. I can't toss it in their kitchen garbage; it'll smell to high heaven. Out of the corner of my eye, I spot the door to the garage. Perfect.

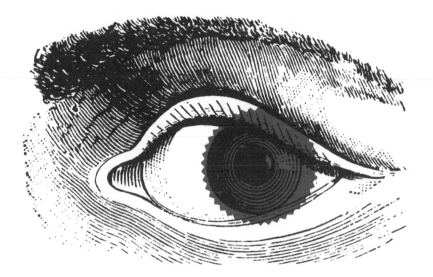

Once inside the garage, I start to gag. The ninety-degree heat mixed with the pungent stench of my soiled underwear brings me to tears. I am covering my mouth with the sleeve of my Reebok T-shirt and running for the garbage can, except there is no garbage can. It must be on the street. Garbage day. Oh, fuck. At this point in time, something happens that I can't quite explain. It is a moment of desperation. One of the most confusing and lowest points of my entire thirteen years. My free hand reaches for a Hoover vacuum cleaner. In a matter of seconds, I rip the bag from the vacuum chamber, stuff my dirty underwear inside the bag, and make a run for the exit.

Here I am, jogging along the side of the house into the Bazalskis backyard, where no one will see me. There in front of me is a perfect spot to toss the murder weapon. A pond. A tiny, algae-filled waterhole where I can finally put these man panties to rest. Ponds are historically the go-to destination for gangsters and lowlifes. I feel like the Al Capone of shitty underwear. I'm about to get away with the biggest crime of my life. For a moment, I look at the sky and smile proudly as I cock my arm back to catapult the bag. I'm drawing upon my Greek ancestry here. I feel like an Olympian. Like I'm about to heave a discus in the ancient games.

The bag leaves my arm and sails in slow motion toward its watery grave. It hits the surface. My heart sinks as the bag stays buoyant. It bobs for a second and then floats off like a tiny, shitty sailboat. Just behind me, I hear the sizzling of a Porterhouse and the dropping of forks. I turn in absolute horror, realizing the Bazalskis are staring at me from their backyard picnic table, thirty feet away. Yes, they just witnessed the entire production. *"Hey, Mr. Nick!"* Mrs. Bazalski laugh-talks. I try to say something, but can't. My new friend and I lock eyes confusedly, and then I do what any boy would do in this situation. I bolt all the way home. **I never saw the family again. I ran into Brian years later at a Target. He was buying a T-shirt, and I swear on my mother's eyes, I was buying underwear.**

THE FIZZ IN MY COKE

Summer is over. It's stinking over.

And I'm going back to school in three days. I can already smell the boy's bathroom. It smells like farts. The teachers are mean. They don't care about us. All they want to do is make money and go home. I don't blame them. Hell, students should get paid too. It's a job, right? I'm fourteen years old. I'm a man. I should just drop out right now and hit the road and never look back. Good-bye to my family, good-bye to my nonpaying bullshit job, and good-bye to the people who pretend to be my friends but talk about how chubby and annoying I am behind my back. "There's a weight limit on that chair, Megalis." That's what Brett Lazowitzsky says every day in math class. He's a fucking asshole. I put on a couple of pounds last winter, and all of a sudden I'm the town fatty. Where will Brett be in ten years? Fat as a house, working a dead-end job at an auto parts store, supporting three kids that might not even be his own, while his girlfriend is sucking the mailman's dick, and he's crying into a lager the size of Ohio at the same bar every single night. I will be eating feta cheese out of a stripper's belly button, while my own song plays full blast in a limousine headed for my sold-out show at Madison Fucking Square Garden. Brett will beg me for VIP passes. He will email me and say, "Remember when we were friends?" And I will have my assistant send him a Xerox of my butthole.

"This is the Worst Mall in America"

my mom says, her bug-eyed sunglasses glued to the road ahead. She's the size of a ladybug, driving a truck that is comically big for a woman her size. Men with tiny penises get Lamborghinis. And short-statured women get trucks the size of school buses. The road is filled with people who shouldn't be driving their particular vehicles. "This mall is a shithole. Worst mall in existence." "Why is this the worst mall? They're all bad. It's Sunglass Huts and JC Penney and a food court," I say. "And speaking of food court, I definitely wanna hit that Chinese place up. Get some egg rolls." I look down at the seat belt cutting into my gut. I could afford to drop a few LBs, but I'm lazy. Unlike my soccer ball–kicking, track-running, pool-swimming classmates, I'm drinking Dr Pepper and drawing comics in my pajamas.

My mom cocks her head and looks down at my gut. She'd never say anything, but she has to know her son is looking like a Cadbury egg. "I'll get you egg rolls, but we're here for your eye exam, so we're goin' there first. If you don't get new glasses in time for school, you're shit out of luck, honey." Not only was I going back to school with a paunch bigger than ever, but I was showing up in glasses. I was like a chubby Buddy Holly. Buddy Hollandaise.

We pull up to the front entrance of the JC Penney slash Target slash Applebee's slash LensCrafters blasting Nelly's "Hot in Herre" over the radio. And no, that's not a misspelling. The guy had the audacity to add an extra r. My mom and I know every word to the song, and we take turns singing each line. For a tiny woman, my mother's vocal cords are rather monstrous. She pushes her voice to its very limit, not really rapping, but rather *yelling* the wildly inappropriate lyrics out the car window. "It's gettin' hot in here, so take off all your clothes!" Then she points at me and it's my turn.

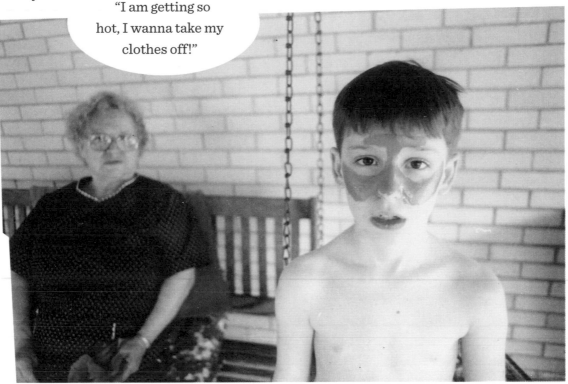

An elderly woman in an oversized T-shirt that simply says OHIO is pushing a shopping cart filled with Yankee Candles and other crap she doesn't need. She passes our truck, and I lock eyes with her as I sing about fame and fucking models. The song gets cut short when my mom pulls her key out of the ignition. "We're late, damn it! Come on!"

Now we're running at supersonic speed through the food court, past all the MSG-injected Chinese chicken that I plan on shoving into my mouth-hole after my eye exam. A cute girl I recognize from school watches my man-boobies bounce wildly under my ill-fitting Cleveland Indians tee as I dash toward the LensCrafters. I pray to God she doesn't know who I am. A skinny little man in a tie is handing out flyers, and he pushes one into our faces. "Twenty percent off all windows and vinyl siding. Perfect for this fall's weather!" he says. My mom is too smart, too quick. "It's a scam. We're not interested," she says as she bolts past him.

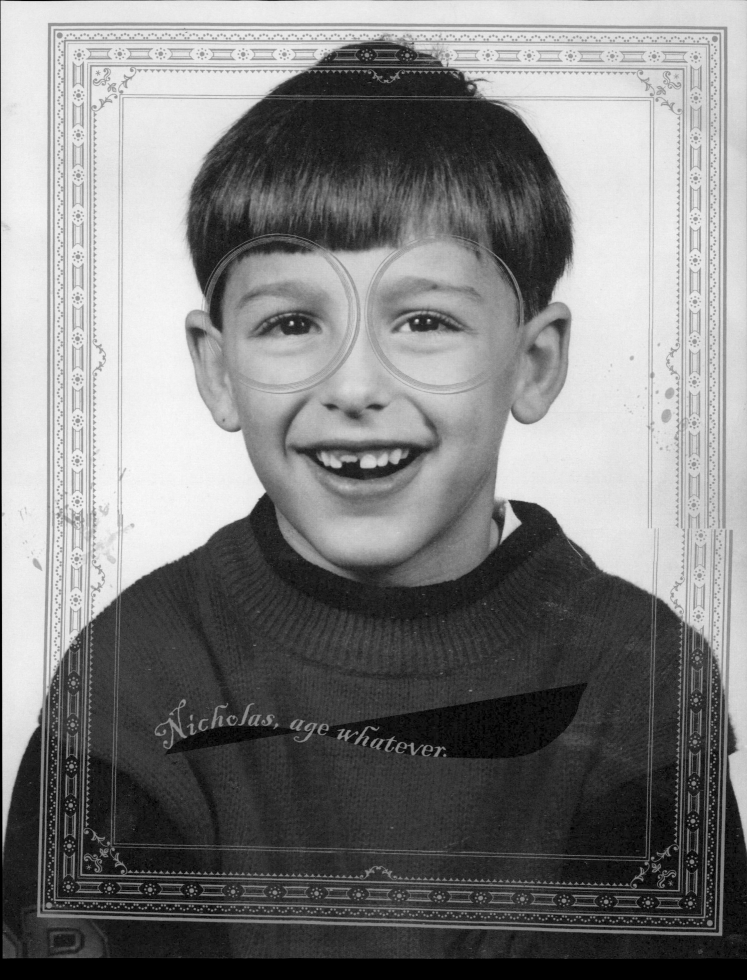

Nicholas, age whatever.

"You must be Nicholas Me*gull*is," the doctor says, butchering my name like she's fucking Ed Gein. I want to correct her, but I have no balls. And plus, what good will it do? This one person out of billions will pronounce my name correctly from here on out? "So, Mr. Me*gull*is, what brings you in today? New pair of glasses, huh?" she says. She's maybe forty-seven. Her face is pretty but made up so heavily that I can't see her real skin. I bet you could dab her makeup off and use it to paint a twelve-foot canvas, maybe a landscape painting, like a waterfall and a tiny cottage somewhere on a mountain. She's got beautiful eyes. I wonder what they've seen. She smells so good. Like a birthday cake. "Let me lean in here and take a look." I am silent while she looks into my eyeballs with a teeny flashlight. I breathe her in without making it obvious. I am fourteen years old and horny pretty much all day long, every single day of every single week. Any woman who so much as glances at me gives me an erection so powerful it could bend steel. If I were a superhero, that would be my ability. Superdick. I can bend the bars of my remote island prison cell and knock my captors unconscious using only the power of my rock-hard boner.

"So what's the damage?" Mom asks as she stands up from the waiting-room chair. She shoves a *Good Housekeeping* magazine under a pile of other magazines. I've seen her do this before. It's because she had nowhere to throw her gum away, so she stuck it between two of the pages. "You have to pick two pages that no one cares about. Like the Viagra ad or some shit," she once told me. "You can't stick it in Jennifer Aniston's interview spread." Mom's wearing a puffy, outdoorsy vest with too many pockets. And her huge sunglasses are sitting atop her tiny head. She's not quite little enough to legally be considered a little person, but she's little as shit.

Walking over to my mom, the doctor says, "Nicholas needs a stronger prescription. I think he should get contacts, because he's at the age where he might not always want to wear glasses. He's so handsome, I really think he should try them." The compliment instantaneously awakens my penis. I do this thing where I try to think of horrible, disgusting, graphic things to tame my erections in social situations. For instance, you imagine a kitten being tied to a bicycle tire and then run over repeatedly as its mangled, blood-soaked fur slaps the ground over and over and over again. Or you think of a high-heeled shoe repeatedly stomping on your testicles, destroying them from the inside, puncturing your balls until they're nothing but flaps of lacerated garbage. See, that works. BONER DEACTIVATED.

The contacts exam is brutal. If you've never purposefully poked yourself in the eyeball before, you probably don't know what it's like to put in contacts. It's just *wrong*. And anybody who says it was easy the first time is either a liar or a twisted bastard who likes touching his wet, sensitive eyeballs. Probably some sadomasochist who lives in his uncle's basement and makes toys out of pubic hair that he collects in public restrooms. *That's* the kind of sicko who likes to finger his own peepers.

It takes me about an hour to not close my eye while I put my finger into it. Then it takes *another* hour to put the contacts into my eyes once I've gotten past the night-mare of touching them. Then, in accordance with Ohio laws, I cannot leave the doc-tor's office without putting them in and taking them out *twice*. Fucking hell. Three hours later, and I leave with beet-red corneas and a prescription for little plastic things that help me see better. Yippee. I can now swim with goggles on. The little kind, not the huge kind that fit over glasses and make you look like an even bigger id-iot. And I can wear sunglasses. Not the sunglasses that clip onto your regular glasses, but the real kind. The kind that gets you laid. The kind that guys on motorcycles wear.

"That was expensive. You better wear these contacts, Boomer," my mom says as we walk toward the food court. I can barely see anything because my eyes are so bloodshot. But from what I can tell, the contacts were a good choice. I have a new attitude already. I feel more confident, like I could waltz into school on Monday and have all the girls asking me out. And Brett Lazowitzsky might even want to hang out after school one day. Maybe he won't treat me like some ant with glasses. Maybe I can be an ant with contacts.

Two egg rolls. One sweet and sour chicken. One large pork fried rice. One large Coke with extra ice. Two handfuls of napkins, way too many napkins. Two handfuls of sauce packets, way too many sauce packets. An extra straw because I hit the straw too hard to remove the wrapper and the plastic cracked. Don't you hate when that happens? My mom is ordering a General Tso's chicken with veggie fried rice and a large Diet Coke. "We have to sit as far away as possible from that clown," Mom says, as we carry our matching green lunch trays. No, she's not being rude. There's an actual clown, in full clown getup, doing tricks and pulling gags in the food court. He's not doing it for free, either. See, that's the worst. When you think something is complimentary and you go along with it, just to humor the person doing it. To be nice and watch the little show. And then they sell you something. Nothing is free. Nothing is magic. Everything on this earth is fueled by money, and everyone is out to make a buck. Even this clown, who is making his way over to our table. My mom is shielding her face, quite literally, with her two miniature hands.

"Oh, God, is he coming over here?" she whispers anxiously. "Oh, shit. Is he? Tell me he's not coming over here. I hate clowns."

The clown approaches. I try not to make eye contact with it. Sorry, *him*. But I can feel *him* smiling at us with his huge painted face. He's in his forties or early fifties, and he's wearing a rainbow tuxedo and oversized red shoes. In his left hand is a fake flower that squirts water. Real original gag. And in his right hand is a clipboard. Red alert. Danger, danger. Red alert, red alert. This seemingly harmless food court jester is about to sign us up for an email chain that will never end. He's going to suck up a half hour of our lunchtime to enroll my mom in some sort of program that will cost my family an exorbitant amount of money every single month for the rest of their lives. Everything is a scam; everyone is out to make a buck. But my mom is two steps ahead. Always two steps ahead. "Listen, I'm sorry, but I don't like clowns. And we don't want to sign up for anything. Thank you," my mom says bluntly. The clown's exaggerated smile turns into an exaggerated frown, and he pouts silently for a few seconds before pantomiming an air-signature. What's worse than a clown? A clown that is also a mime.

"We aren't signing up for anything. We are eating our lunch, and I don't like clowns. Sorry, have a beautiful day." My mom has balls. Big, fat, droopy balls.

And this clown is barking up the wrong testicle. He sets the clipboard down on the table and takes a few steps back in his big shoes. He reaches into an imaginary hat and pulls out an imaginary rabbit. He pets the fake rabbit and then does a little dance. My mom is fucking *livid*. She tries her damnedest to ignore the little show, laser-focusing in on my face. "So, how do your new contacts feel, Boomer?" I love when she calls me Boomer. It's just a cute little nonsense thing she's called me my whole life. "Yeah, they feel good now. It took some getting used to but . . ." I can see she isn't paying attention. How could she? A six-foot-tall psycho with a red nose and a wig is doing the fucking Cabbage Patch in his stupid shoes. I can feel my mom's anger brewing across the table. It's hotter than the garlic-chili dipping sauce for my egg rolls.

"Okay, listen." She shoots up from her chair, sending it flying. The clown stops dancing midthrust, and his exaggerated smile melts off of his face. Giddy, cartoon fun has just kicked into another gear—real, actual fear. He gulps and clutches his clipboard to his chest. "We don't want to sign up for anything. We don't want a show. I want to eat lunch with my son. And I don't like clowns." Then something unbelievable happens. The clown speaks. "Sorry, ma'am. I work for the bank, and they make me do this. I don't like clowns either," he says, shrugging sadly. How quickly a popular dance routine can descend into crippling, depressing darkness. My mom looks at me and looks back at the clown, and then looks at me again and back at the clown once more. She's sad, and I'm sad too. Everyone is sad, damn it! Why does he have to break our hearts like this? She doesn't say much. She just grabs the clipboard and signs it. Doesn't even read the information. She just blindly signs it and gives him a hug. The clown smiles and does a little goofy bow.

It is the strangest moment of the day. I would say it was the strangest moment of my life, but my life is a whirlwind of weirdness, so I can't be sure.

We can barely walk. The MSG is working its way into our bloodstreams. I can already feel my fingers getting fatter, and my gut is making sounds I've never heard before. That's food-court Chinese food for you. Might as well just feed us diarrhea. Platefuls of fresh, piping-hot diarrhea. Because that's what it's going to turn

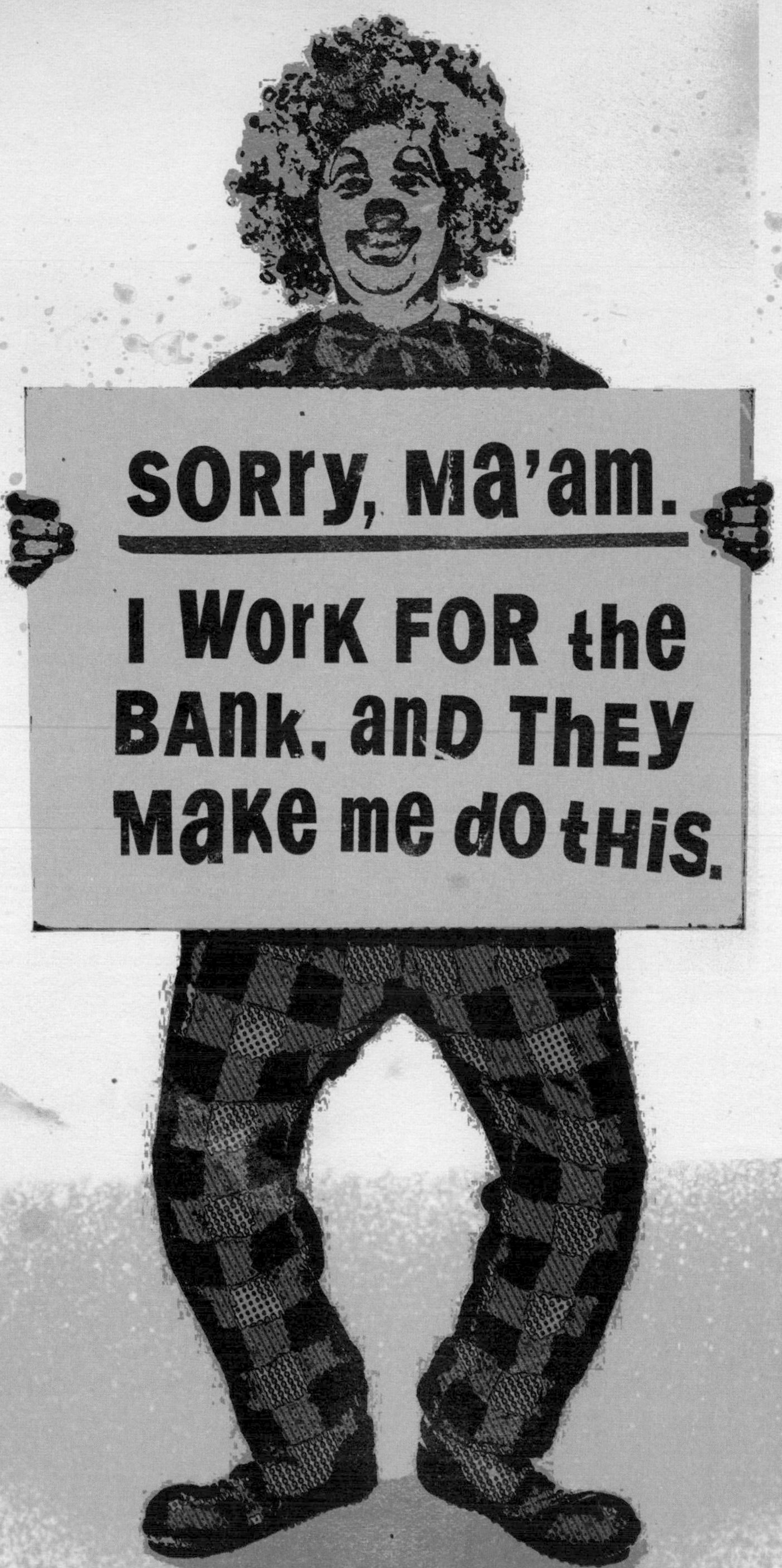
SORRY, MA'AM.
I WORK FOR the BANK, anD THEY MAKE me dO tHIS.

into anyway. As we make our way toward the exit, I decide I haven't had enough food. Even though the brass button on my blue jeans is about to pop like a cork on New Year's Eve, I could still go for some dessert. My mom and I have a form of ESP that can only be described as foodcentric. She knows when I'm hungry, and she knows what for. She glances over at the Auntie Anne's pretzels kiosk, then looks at me with a smile as wide as Ohio. "Let's do it."

The kiosk is a brilliant thing. The ultimate in American laziness. A store without doors, without floor space. A tiny little stand where you can just buy something and get the fuck out of there in a matter of seconds. No walking around, painstakingly deciding what you want to waste your money on. It's been picked out *for* you. Swipe your card and stuff your face. Genius. My mom and I wait in line behind an Indian family and eavesdrop on their incessant bickering. It's hilarious. The dad is upset at the daughter for not texting him the directions to the mall, and the mother is mad at the dad for not texting the son about the shirt that he wanted. It's just a clusterfuck of neglectful text messaging. "Don't you ever think maybe you should text your father the directions, Anisha? I looked up and down the world for two hours!"

My mom is scrutinizing the Auntie Anne's menu like it's a history exam. "I don't know what I want. I kind of want the chocolate-dipped pretzels, but I also want the cheese-stuffed. What should I get? Shit, shit, shit!" she asks me. I myself am torn between the various diabetes-causing treats. It is the hardest decision I'll have to make all day. My life must be pretty cozy. Then a voice. A voice from around the other side of the kiosk. It sounds like a young man, hawking pretzel samples. Score! "Mom, they're giving out samples over there. Let's go."

We turn the corner of the kiosk. The voice is coming from a man in an electric wheelchair. I'm not certain, but I think he has muscular dystrophy. He is almost completely paralyzed except for his mouth, which he uses to bite down on a button that moves his chair. His arms are twisted impossibly at the joints, and his legs are bent toward each other. His limbs are the size of a small child's, but he's easily ten years older than me. He's wearing a Cleveland Indians hat and an Auntie Anne's shirt with a badge that says his name: WILL. The purple marker that spells out his name is surrounded in gold stickers and smiley faces. He's got thin blond hair and a bit of a goatee. He glances over and then bites his button to move the chair to face us. "Hi, guys. Would you like to try our new cheese-stuffed pretzel bites?"

My mother doesn't even pause for a second to consider. She walks right up to Will, leans in close, and says, "Don't tell my son, but I think I love Auntie Anne's pretzels more than him." Will cracks a smile and looks over at me. "I won't tell him if you buy my pretzels!" he says. She grabs a few pretzel bites from a plastic tray that's attached to Will's chair and hands one to me. I take a bite of the chewy, cheesy bread and try my best not to stare. I'm just so sad for him. It's just so unfair. I want to cry.

"Damn, these are good as *gold*!" my mom says.

"Aren't these good, Boomer?" she asks, turning to face me. "Yeah, so good!" I say. Will's chair is covered in stickers. Stickers from all over the country, it seems. The largest sticker on the side of his chair reads NEW JERSEY-THE GARDEN STATE. My mom squints to read it. Her eyes are so goddamn bad. But she's so stubborn, she wouldn't get her eyes checked when we were just at the doctor. "New Jersey? That's great! Do you have family there? I love that sticker. I have some family there."

A little boy, maybe four years old, makes his way for the free samples, and his mother grabs his arm. "Honey, those aren't for you." She looks at Will with nervous eyes. She hauls her son off, and as they walk away, she glances over her shoulder to catch another glimpse of the man in the electric wheelchair. It's the same look a small child has when it's face-to-face with an animal. Fear. My mom keeps talking to Will. They're somehow deep in a conversation about New Jersey, and apparently Will's mother grew up there. My mother talks about her second cousin's beach house

SEAL OF THE STATE OF NEW JERSEY.

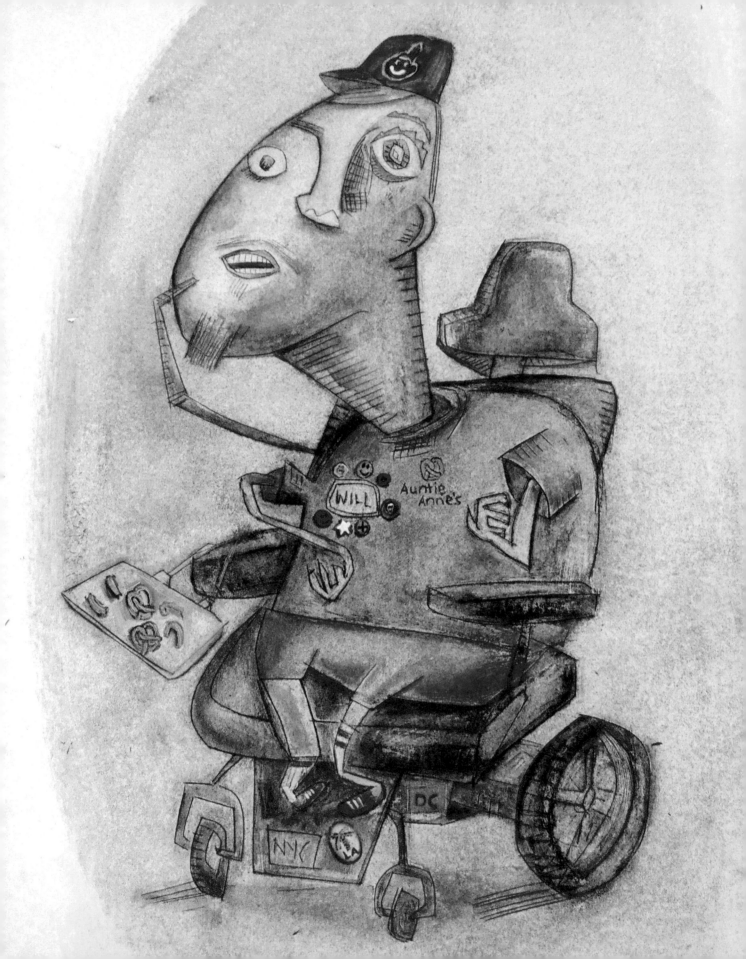

on the Jersey Shore and how we are never invited there because of some stupid incident that happened years and years ago that she can't even remember. She reaches in for another cheesy pretzel bite.

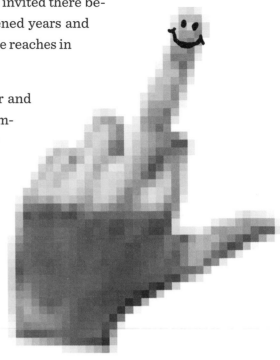

Two guys with beautifully parted hair and suits that probably cost more than our family vehicle pass by the kiosk. I can't hear what they're saying, but they're pointing their manicured fingers at the man in the electric wheelchair and chuckling. Assholes. It stings. It angers me deep in my gut. I imagine them both in wheelchairs, paralyzed from the neck down. I wonder what they'd chuckle about then. My mom notices the dickbags gawking at Will, and she offers them up a free sample of her middle finger.

"So, Will, are you always here? We gotta come see you next time we're in for Nick's glasses," my mom says. "Well, I'm here three days a week. And I would love to see you guys again. I gotta try some of your famous meatloaf. Bring it in next time. Oh, and Denise . . . call me Wheelie. That's what my friends call me." In the past four minutes, my mother and this total stranger have bonded over something as mundane as cheesy pretzel bites. She didn't get down on her knee and speak loudly at him like he was a deaf baby. She didn't ogle him like he was a science experiment. She didn't look the other way when she saw him. She treated him like a human being. I know this sounds

strange, but today, in the Running Rivers Mall, in Akron, Ohio, my life has changed. I have realized that although someone's situation may be unfortunate, we are all just living. Will isn't in a bed somewhere, sleeping the day away like a sad sack of shit. He's just playing the hand he was dealt. And handing out pretzel bites at the mall. It's a safe bet that Will's got a better attitude than 90 percent of the population. And even though he may look different from me or sound different from you, it doesn't mean a goddamn thing.

My mom, a dangerously explosive firecracker of a woman, is also somehow the kindest person I have ever met. She'll kick your ass and hand it to you. She will cut your testicles off, toss them in a blender, and switch on the "pulverize" setting. She will run you over with her truck that is also about the size of a small house. But she'll also hit the pause button on her own life for a minute, just to ask you how yours is going. My mom never went out of her way to teach me a lesson about how to treat others. She just did her thing, and I noticed how it impacted people. There is nothing, and I mean absolutely *nothing*, more important than making someone smile. Even if it's just once a day for two measly seconds. Life is little tiny moments all strung together. Why not make someone's little tiny moment just a little tiny bit better?

We pull into the school parking lot on a cool Monday morning at the end of August and rattle every other car with our subwoofer. I'm about to walk into my first day of ninth grade, and we are blasting Missy Elliott's new song "Work It" at 7:30 in the morning. All the windows are down, and my mom is screaming, "See my ass and my hips, don't ya?" A man who may or may not be my principal is staring at us from the entrance. He gives a confused wave, and I wave back. My mom turns the music down as I unbuckle my seat belt and open my passenger door. She puts her tiny little arm around my neck, and she pulls me in and says, "You are going to do great. I love you more than all the blades of grass on the earth. You are the fizz in my Coke." She kisses the top of my head, and I shut the door.

As I make my way through the doors with a packed lunch and a little bit of a gut, I hear my mom's radio blasting obscenities as she pulls away. My buddy Brian Dallerman taps me on the shoulder and says,

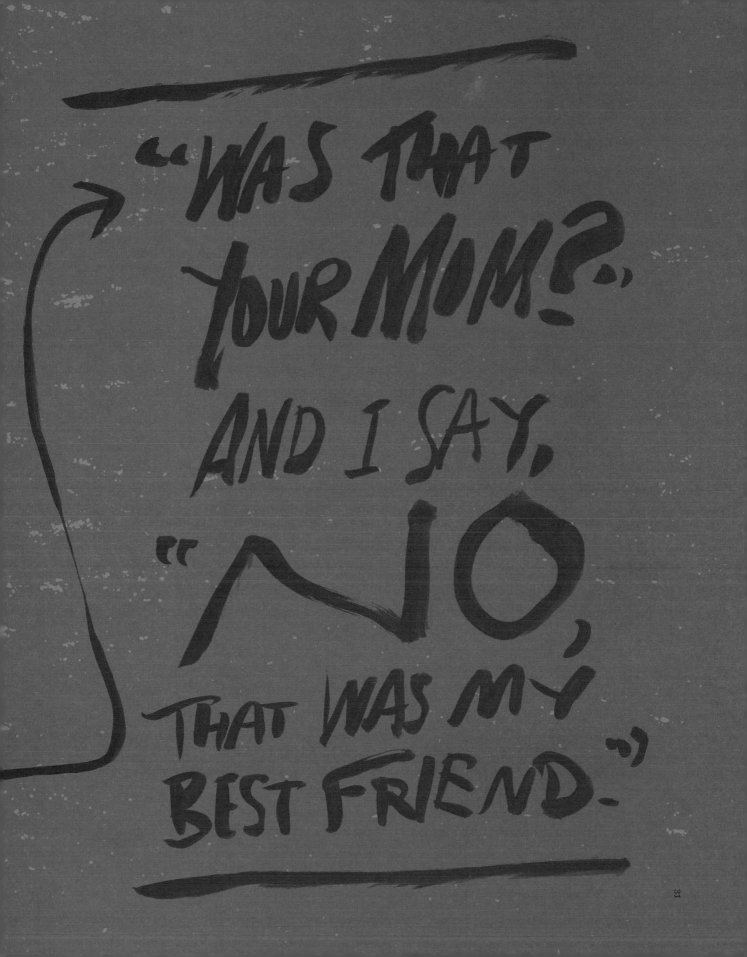

THE SMELLIEST KID I'VE EVER KNOWN

I wish you had been there to smell him. John Bunyan the Onion.

He stood as high as my nipples and he smelled like garbage. I met him on the first day of fourth grade. He came out of nowhere like a bolt of smelly lightning. We bonded when he reached into his pants pocket and showed me a crumpled-up picture of *X-Files* actress Gillian Anderson wearing a bikini. He apparently carried it around in his unwashed pants every single day. He also wore the same shirt every single day—a permanently off-white Gap V-neck, ill-fitting over his skinny frame and stained brown from sweat and chocolate pudding. I only ever saw him eat pudding, swear to Jesus. Nothing else. The kid ate it for breakfast and lunch, and he never paid for it. He'd swipe a pudding cup when the cafeteria ladies weren't looking.

I was the only friend he had. His odor kept away humans, animals, and plants. At lunch, he sat alone at one end of a cafeteria table, across from the worst group of girls on the face of the planet. They were just miserable. They'd throw milk cartons at John while he licked his pudding cup spotless. "Ewwww . . . Bunyan the Onion! Bunyan the Onion!" they'd chant. I wanted to individually smack the shit out of them. Especially Brianna Briggs. The lead pot-stirrer. She was a demon. You could just see

BUNYON THE ONION

the evil in her black little eyes. She had Ronald McDonald hair, too many freckles for a human face, and a voice that sounded like broken glass being shoved up a cat's asshole. I started sitting with John because I felt sorry for him. I usually sat alone too, so I figured we could team up and be losers together. The first day I sat with him, he devised this sinister plan to cup his fart and send it sailing across the table, right into the thick of the evil girl table. I didn't understand the logistics. But John showed me. "Look, dude, it's easy. You cup your hand over your butthole and fart into it, and then throw it!" he said, cheerful as a chipmunk. I can still hear his raspy *Little Rascals* voice. High-pitched and goofy. Like a windup monkey.

John lobbed the fart across the table while I hid my face in my sweatshirt. The girls stopped chirping and started sniffing. "*Ewwwwwwwww!*" Ronald McDonald girl shrieked. I was floored. I had never met someone who possessed such mastery over the art of fart tossing. He chucked his gas at those girls from twelve feet away. It seemed impossible. I was convinced that John had a special form of toxic gas that was dense enough to be thrown. He was a fart terrorist. The Unabomber of Anal Belching.

One afternoon, I invited the Onion over to my house for snacks and a Gillian Anderson session. I guess after a few weeks of sitting next to him in the lunchroom, I had gotten used to his stench. I mean, he still made me physically sick. Like, sick enough to want to vomit sometimes. But I had very few friends, and I really wanted to look at Gillian Anderson's titties. So I sucked it up. At school, my teachers started to think it was me who smelled. John was rubbing off on me, literally. If he put his arm on me for two seconds, my shirt would smell like dog shit for the next twelve hours. Mrs. Henderson actually went out of her way to have a "talk" with John and me after math class one day. "Listen, boys. You need to start to take showers more often. I don't want to be your mother, but your mothers aren't doing a good job." Those were her actual words. The bitch thought I stank too.

We open the door to my house, and I take off my shoes. John leaves his on. "Dude, can you take those off?" I ask him, pointing to his poop-brown, hand-me-down kicks. He nods and kicks them off. Immediately, I'm nauseated. The stench is appalling. It smells almost exactly like the raccoon my dad found in our gutters the summer before. Only slightly worse. I regret my decision and beg him to put them back on. He laughs, "Sorry about the smell, dude." Dude, dude, dude, dude, dude. That's how we speak. Our combined vocabularies consist of maybe eight words:

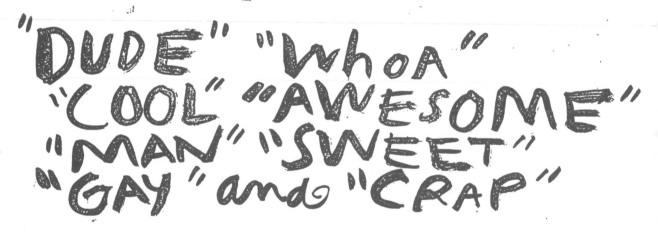

"DUDE" "WhoA"
"COOL" "AWESOME"
"MAN" "SWEET"
"GAY" and "CRAP"

My mother enters the living room to meet our pungent guest. She's visibly distraught. She gives me a look, and we share a little mother-to-son ESP. Kinda like the little kid and the black guy from *The Shining*. "This kid smells really bad," she eye-talks. "I know, Mom," I answer nonverbally. She snaps out of it and smiles at John. "Hi, I'm Mrs. Megalis. Pleasure to meet you. Do you guys want to eat dinner outside?" And I know she's offering that we have our dinner outside, as opposed to inside, because John smells like a corpse. "Sure! I want chicken nuggets!" he says, like a little bastard. The balls on this kid. My mom clenches her fist, and as politely as she can, says, "Well, we don't have chicken nuggets. We have spaghetti. And that's what you'll be having."

A few hours pass. We are seated at the plastic kids' table outside on the back porch of my house. I'm drunk on strawberry Kool-Aid. John is licking pasta sauce off the plate like he's never had a meal in his life. And it hits me hard. I don't know why I hadn't put it together before, but I get it now. John is dirt poor. His clothes, his lack of hygiene, his tendency to steal pudding every day in the cafeteria. My mom definitely knew it when she met him. Which is why she's bringing him plate after plate of spaghetti. She always helps people out. Trick-or-treaters come to our house because my mom hands out king-sized candy bars and cans of soda. She's a giver; it's her nature. My mom didn't want John stinking up our kitchen, but she's happy to stuff him full of as much pasta as he can devour outside.

The sun is starting to set, and John excuses himself from the plastic table. "You wanna walk me back to my house? I have something I wanna show you." I agree, and we start on the short walk down the hill to his neighborhood. See, John's neighborhood is only blocks from my own. But it's vastly different. A separate universe. It's a land of malnourished dogs, loud fights in the middle of the street, and shacks that can barely be considered houses. It's eye-opening and frightening. John and I walk side-by-side as he points out all of his friends' houses. "Tony lives there. He's the fattest kid in the neighborhood," he says. "And over there, that's Alec Mackelroy's house. He's albino. And his dad has a potbelly pig for sale." The sign in the front yard says it all: PIG FOR SALE.

John lives on this gigantic hill. It's so steep, you can barely walk down it. It's like a 90-degree angled staircase in an M.C. Escher drawing. All of the houses are built sideways into the incline, and I wonder how they can possibly pour milk into their cereal in the morning. Does it all just spill out onto the wall? John stops in front of his house and whispers into my ear, "Stay outside, dude. I have a present for you." I stand in the driveway, freaked. He opens the screen door to the sounds of barking and bottles falling all over the place. I can hear some guy yelling. Sounds like his dad. "Johnny, where the fuck you been?" he screams. John runs out of the house with a big garbage bag filled with something and hands it to me. "Take this. They're yours," he says, and runs back into the house. The bag is pretty heavy, so I heave it over my shoulder. I start the slow trek back up the hill, in the dark, anxious to see what the hell John gave me.

It's hard to rush into my house with a bag full of shit. My mom is too smart. So I sneak into the garage. I'm desperate to open it now. As I untie the knot, and the light of the garage hits the inside of the bag, I can make out the shape of a woman's bare breast. I reach my hand into the bag and push the contents around. It's dusty. Dirty. Feels like books. No, these are magazines. I turn the bag upside down and shake it empty. There, on the floor of my garage, are two dozen of the filthiest smut-rags ever published. John's dad's collection of vintage *Hustler* magazines. The porn jackpot. I pick one out of the pile and look at the date. August 1981. Eight years before I was born. The big-haired blonde woman on the cover is spreading her legs but you can't see her privates on account of the word *HOT* blocking it out in big red letters. I'm disappointed for a moment, thinking that these magazines might be censored. I flip open to the first page, and my brain explodes all over the garage. My eyes take in the

nasty, hairy mass of flesh and veins. I had never even seen a nipple outside of my mother's, and here I am staring into the unkempt bush of Ms. Stella Porkright.

Cocks that look like monsters. These aren't penises. I have a penis. My dad has a penis. I've seen penises in paintings. The *things* in this magazine are hideous. They hang to the floor like a third leg. Uncircumcised, venous beasts. The women don't look happy either. They're making these pained faces while the guys stick these things inside of their things. I'm humiliated and uncomfortably turned on. I have a knot in my stomach and a boner in my shorts. My friend Mason once told me on the bus that a vagina was a "butt in the front," and this magazine is destroying everything I thought I knew about vaginas. These don't look like butts. They look like aliens. Or like alien mouths. Some of these women even appear to have teeth in their vaginas. I'm flipping through the pages too quickly to notice, but I think I saw some teeth. And don't get me started on buttholes. I must have seen at least ten in the first few pages. All wrinkly and brown, like an old lady's mouth after eating a lemon.

I've seen enough. This is just wrong. That smelly little troublemaker dumped all of this filth into my life. Look, I love naked ladies. But I'm not ready for this level of debauchery. I like the *idea* of nudity more than the oily, unshaved *reality* of it. I bag up the porn and shove it under my dad's car. I go inside, wash my hands in the kitchen sink, and my unaware mom comes downstairs to scoop me some nighttime ice cream. I'm nauseously eating spoonfuls of Rocky Road and praying to God that my mother can't see the horror in my eyes. Little does she know that my innocence is gone, thanks to the stinkbug who just hours ago had sucked down her famous spaghetti.

The next morning, my dad backs out of our driveway to take me down to my bus stop. Still in a stupor after last night's events, I hug my dad, close the door to the car, and get on the waiting bus. I pop a squat next to John Bunyan the Onion, in the only open seat. He smells worse than ever before. Like he bathed in human feces. "Did you enjoy your gift?" he asks with a grin. I smile nervously. "Yeah, dude, thanks," I say. As the bus starts to pull away, I look out the window and see my dad's car driving off in the opposite direction. I then see the big black bag, half-ripped apart, dragging behind my dad's car, spilling sex all over the neighborhood. **Pieces of titties, vaginas, and veiny cocks dance in the wind like little pornographic snowflakes.**

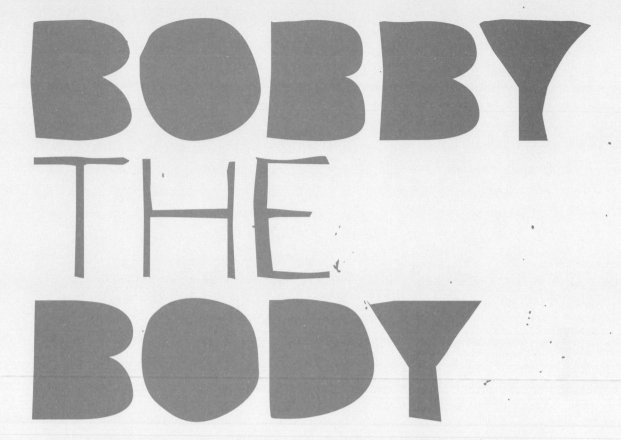

BOBBY THE BODY

I pull up to my girlfriend's dorm on a bike I found in the garbage.

Two nights ago, drunk off my ass on bodega beer and walking around Brooklyn, I spotted the Huffy bike on a pile of rat-infested trash bags. The tires weren't flat, so I rescued it. But it's a little bent, and I kinda have to sit sideways to get it to pedal right. That's okay, though. I'm young and broke, and I can sit sideways on a broken bike if I have to.

My girlfriend just moved into this apartment building as part of Kent State University's New York City semester. The fashion program that she's in sends all the girls to the Big Apple for four months. Most of the girls have never been to New York, including my girlfriend, Catherine. The building is atrocious, even from the outside. I take one look at it and know it's a dump. The ugly poop-brown brick. The front awning ripped to shreds from years of neglect and winter ice. As I chain my bike to a signpost near the entrance, a bag lady and her dog recline on a heap of foul, blackened blankets, soaked with the world-famous New York City aroma of urine with a dash of feces.

It's late August, and an end-of-summer heat wave is upon us. What a perfect time to smell like shit, with the sun baking it nice and hot for everyone to enjoy.

This is Chelsea—a primarily residential neighborhood on Manhattan's West Side. Like all of New York, there are beautiful sections and absolutely rancid sections, where God himself would tremble. But thanks to rapid gentrification, by the time this book is published, there will be a hundred more Best Buys and approximately seven thousand more Chipotles. So you won't have to worry about that. The sprawling flower gardens, tree-lined walkways along the pier, the perfectly manicured parks, and pristine French eateries. Georgian-style architecture rubbing shoulders with Gothic-style architecture. A cornucopia of lavishness and upscale urban living. But what's so great about New York City is that in the middle of all of this grace, in the secret garden next door to the petite bakery where pound cake is seventeen dollars a slice, stands a man pissing himself, wearing a dress made out of deflated balloons and aluminum foil. Outside the Plaza Hotel on Fifth Avenue and Central Park South, where guests are enjoying cocktails and casual conversation, is a horse taking a steaming shit and a woman with her breasts completely exposed, screaming at the sky about the second coming of Jesus Christ.

This hodgepodge of wealth and poverty, prosperity and crippling mental illness, is what made me want to live here in the first place. When their limousines are late, the richest, most powerful men in the world have to ride the train with the Dunkin' Donuts employees. We are all the same. And that is so beautiful I could cry.

"Hey, you're early!" Catherine says with a smile. Always so pleasant, always so happy to see me. Even with me soaked in sweat, she gives me a kiss. Her long, black, coffee-colored hair dances off the back of her neck in the path of the air conditioner. We sit down at a tiny table and stare at each other through the visible heat. It's the sex stare. The metaphysical entangling of emotions, exchanged without opening one's mouth. The look that says, "Let's rip each other's clothes off and do it on the floor."

"Do you want anything to eat?" she asks, shaking off the intimacy. "No, I'm good," I say. Catherine stands up and gives me the grand tour of the place with one simple gesture of her open arms. She turns, does a 360, and laughs, "So, what do you think?" If I cock my head just a little, I can see the entire apartment. It's one room. A bunk

bed against a scuffed white wall, a closet-sized bathroom, and a living room/kitchen combo that consists of a teeny dining table and a stovetop. The only people who would find any comfort in this claustrophobic living space are astronauts and prisoners.

"It's like a cupboard with a microwave," I joke. Catherine does a cute little shrug and hands me a menu for a Chinese restaurant. "They deliver. Isn't that awesome? We don't even have to leave," she tells me. As if I want to spend any more time than I have to in this shoebox. Granted, delivery is definitely a novel thing for us. New York City is famed for its speedy food shipments. There are so many restaurants in Chelsea alone that it would be impossible to eat at them all, even if you lived ten lifetimes. This is mainly because the restaurants get so many health-code violations that they shut down almost as quickly as they open. (I won't get into the nasty details, but let's just say the chicken isn't chicken.)

Catherine calls in an order for veggie lo mein and something called "Happy Family," which is basically just a pile of shrimp that haven't been deveined and pieces of unidentifiable meat chunks in a thick, translucent sauce. We sweat in front of the air conditioner as we eat our meal. My T-shirt is stuck so tightly to my torso, it's merged with my own skin. I drink warm beer from a 40-ounce bottle, but Catherine doesn't drink. She hasn't had a single sip of alcohol since seventh grade, when her friend forced her to try a Mike's Hard Lemonade at a party. So I do the drinking for both of us.

When I'm all nice and toasty on Colt 45 and MSG, I'm ready to explore the building. "Let's go to the roof!" I suggest excitedly. Outside the only window in the whole apartment, the sun is almost fully gone, leaving a pinkish-orange glow on the horizon. The stuff of dreams. New York City summers are hot and stinky but absolutely enchanting. The elevator is being worked on, so we take the stairs. But when we get to the twentieth floor, the stairs run out, and we have to climb a rusty, loose stepladder propped up against a wall. I make Catherine climb first so that I can catch her if she loses her footing, and also because I wanna look up her skirt. She should have kicked me in the fucking head.

Catherine pushes the latch open on the ceiling, and out we go into the night. The view is just crazy. One of my first experiences on a proper New York City rooftop. Skyscrapers poke up through the smog and sparkle all crystal-like with their tiny window lights. The sound of car horns, broken arguments in various languages, and police sirens all around us. Catherine and I partake in some inappropriate canoodling as the city reverberates.

What an incredible town, I think to myself. So many ecosystems doing their own thing, all at once. Explosive life pulsating all around, never ceasing. Relentless. Then there are moments like these, where you can pause and close your eyes and just bury your nose in your girlfriend's hair and smell it. And that's all you want to do. Because you're finally free for a second, and you aren't at war. Just for a second.

New York City is drawing me further into its clutches. I can feel myself falling in love with *buildings*, for Christ's sake.

I am bewitched by this magnificent hellhole, and I know it'll only get more intense. "Let's go inside. It's getting chilly," Catherine suggests. I agree, push myself off the tar-paper roof, and make my way down the rusty ladder. "You should come up here and draw," I say, underneath Catherine, looking up her skirt. "Yeah, that would be nice," she says. The top-floor hallway is dimly lit by one flickering lightbulb with no fixture. Just a bare bulb making this awful high-pitched electrical buzz. As we walk down the stairs, I listen to all the muffled racket from inside people's apartments.

"You never fuck me! You never fuck me!" an elderly woman shouts. Another flight of stairs. Caribbean dance music thumping through the dirty walls. Another flight of stairs. The thick smell of curry and marijuana smoke. A young black girl crying in the hallway with a joint in one hand and her cellphone in the other. "What the fuck you looking at?" she hollers. "Nothing. Sorry," Catherine mumbles.

"I'm going to the bodega to get some more beer," I announce as we enter her miniature living quarters. She's not too happy, but a man's gotta drink some beer. So I grab a wad of *her* money off the counter when she's not looking, and I scram. Drunkenly walking down the stairs, singing Radiohead very loudly, I almost can't hear the cries. An older man. I can hear it now. I stop in my tracks and listen. "Bobby, where are you? Bobby? Bobby! I broke my leg, Bobby!" he moans. First off, why nobody else could hear this is beyond me. How long was he calling for help? What the hell is going on? I pinpoint the source of the howling and put my head against his door. "Bobby, is that you? I broke my leg, Bobby! I fell and broke my goddamn leg!" The door is actually not closed the whole way. I can kind of poke my face in. "Sir? Is everything all right?" I ask. "Get Bobby. I broke my leg!" he says. Something is blocking the door, and I can't push it open. I can make out a very skinny figure lying on the ground, smoking a cigarette next to the door. He's maybe eighty years old. Incredibly gaunt. Skeletal. And he's only wearing a pair of stained white underwear, sagging below his bony hip. His beard is straggly and white, and his bald head is spotted with moles and discolorations. Behind him are literally hundreds of books, stacked

in piles to the ceiling. A radio is turned on in the background, playing something that sounds like Bing Crosby. "You're my baby, my little darling girl," the crooner sings through static, as the elderly man takes a hit of his cigarette. The stench of Marlboro smoke is overwhelming. It burns my eyes. "I can't open the door. You're blocking it, sir. I'm going to call an ambulance." "Bobby, where the fuck is Bobby!" he curses at me. "I don't know, sir, but you need to calm down and stay put." His tiny arm reaches up and pushes the door completely closed, and *click*. He locks it. He locks the fucking door. Great, now nobody can help him. The fire department is going to have to break the door down to get him out. I dial 911 and tell them that an elderly man has broken his leg. As I'm talking to the dispatcher, the old man keeps wailing on and on about Bobby. "Where is Bobby?" I ask through the door. "Bobby is next door, goddamn it! I broke my goddamn leg!" he yells.

Okay, finally some actual information. I'll just go and get this Bobby character and he can help us. Maybe he's the landlord. Who knows. I can't tell which door is "next door," because there's a door to my left that looks like an apartment, and a smaller door in between that looks like a janitor's closet. The door that looks like an apartment is shut. I knock hard, and nothing. Ring the buzzer, and nothing. I glance over at the janitor's closet, and there's a blue hue emanating from under the door. Somebody's in there. I press my cheek against it to listen, and the door opens. Just like that. I step into the room, almost against my will. As if I'm being beckoned by this eerie blue light.

The gentle hum of static. A tiny portable TV sits on a nightstand, tuned to the snow channel, and an obese body lies in a tiny bed. Those are the only things in the room. Because nothing else would fit. The entire apartment is the length of the bed and the fat man that's in it. There aren't any lights on, but I can see well enough with the light from the TV. His left arm hangs off the mattress, and the other is propped up uncomfortably above his head, rested at the elbow against the wall. He is facing the ceiling with his mouth open. "Bobby?" I whisper. I rap my fingers against the open door. "Bobby?" Outside in the hallway, I can hear the old man shouting again. "Tell Bobby I broke my goddamn leg!" Bobby is still. Too still. His bloated gut doesn't go up and down when he breathes. Because he's not breathing. "Did you find Bobby?" the old man inquires.

I calmly close the door and step into the hallway. My hands are rattling.

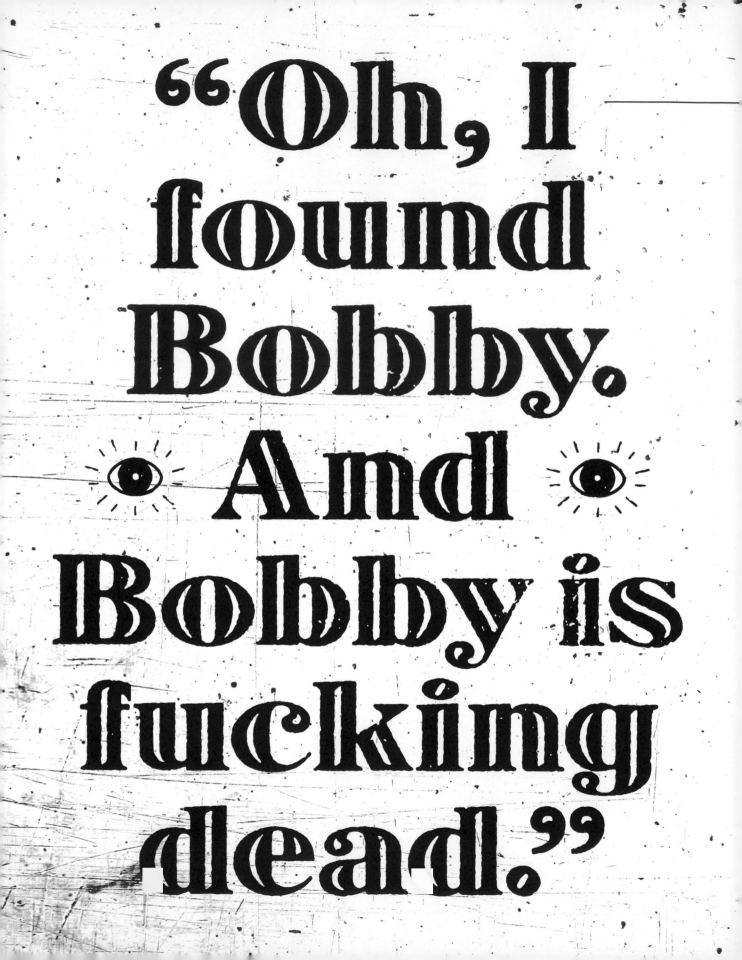

The paramedics arrive to rescue the old man, and I stand in the corridor, waiting to tell them. "Break her open, Peter." "Got it, Danny." They destroy the lock using a fire extinguisher and finally get to the old man, who is still lying on the floor with a cigarette butt and no pants on. A third guy comes up the stairs with a stretcher, and they carefully pick up the tiny man and get him out of the room. Now's my chance. I gotta tell these guys about Bobby.

"Ex . . . excuse me . . . ," I stutter. "I found a guy next door . . . there's . . . there's a guy next door who's . . . who's dead, I think?" I tell the burly paramedic. "Do you wanna go in and . . . and look at it?" He stares at me blankly and says in a thick Brooklyn accent, "Nah. That ain't our job." The *fuck*? This guy is literally telling me he wants *nothing* to do with the *corpse* I found. I am so dumbfounded, I just stand there in a stupor while they take the old man away.

Over the next five days, my girlfriend would notice an increasingly horrific odor. The smell of death. If I had to describe it, it would be a combination of human feces and rotten rib eye. Just unbearable. Filling the entire building with a stench so putrid and evil that we couldn't bear to stay indoors. Then one afternoon, as Catherine and I are eating ice cream cones on the corner, a van pulls up marked CORONER. Two guys in plastic yellow coats and yellow gloves get out of the van and enter the building. I run upstairs to grab Catherine's jacket because it's starting to rain. And on my way back down, I catch a glimpse of Bobby's bloated, blue body through his open door. His clothes are soaked in strange orange fluids, and his arm is permanently cocked in the awkward position it was when I found him almost a week earlier. A fly lands on his yellowed eyeball. And the smell is so strong, I have to get the hell out of there. Back outside the building, the men are loading the body bag into the van. A small crowd of tourists takes photos. I lean in to say something as they slam the van doors closed. "You know, I told the paramedics about this five days ago. I'm the one who found him. Do you need to ask me any questions?"

They both stare at me like I'm a moron, and the fat one laughs and says, "Nah. That ain't our job."

TOTAL ROCK'N'ROLL DOMINATION

We pack into the van like sardines for the third time that day after a fifteen-minute break to stretch our legs and take stinky dumps in a truck-stop bathroom. My drummer, Timmy, is the last to get in the van. He walks leisurely across the parking lot on his cellphone, probably flirting with some girl from the town before. He gets into the car with a grin on his face and hangs up the phone. "Dudes, that girl wants me. So bad." The smell of truck-stop gasoline and human feces is still stuck on his pants; he climbs into the back of our tiny tour van and slides the door shut.

"You're never gonna see her again, dude. She lives in Denver. And plus, she's not a girl. She's a *woman*. A forty-year-old *woman*, Timmy," Rich says from the far back-seat. Rich is a realistic man. The most reasonable and normal out of all of us. And he's deeply, deeply regretting joining this band. The minute the kid got in the car, he was already crying into his hands and asking God, "*Why?*" It's not that Timmy or I or our tour manager are bad guys. It's just that riding in a van for a month with no air conditioning, no room to stretch your legs, and the nauseating fumes of farts and unwashed clothing can be a nightmare for anyone with a functioning brain. And Rich has the most functional brain out of all of us.

"I'm serious, Timmy. She had a gut too. Like, it hung over her pants. Her stomach looked like a grocery bag of spilled beef. She lives in Denver, and she has a gut and probably children, dude. She's forty," Rich says, trying to bring Timmy down to earth. Timmy still has a huge grin. He puts his headphones on. On tour, headphones are an escape from the sweaty, suffocating madness of everything. You put on your headphones and you listen to jazz and just float off into a magical land where you aren't eating Taco Bell, and you don't have indigestion from the Taco Bell you ate the night before, and the Taco Bell from the night before that. Driving from Ohio to Los Angeles, fueled by caffeine, marijuana, alcohol, and fast food is something I would never wish on anyone. And at the same time, it's something that I would *absolutely* wish on everyone. It's a lethal combination of fun and anxiety. A fucked-up, monthlong binge of excess, psychosis, and guitars.

We pull into the venue parking lot at around 6 p.m. on the hottest day of the entire tour. Tucson, Arizona. The Devil's asshole. The whole place smells like death and gasoline. With the windows rolled down and my head out the passenger window like a beaten dog, I savor every drop of sweat that cools my face. The four of us are shirtless and exhausted from an eleven-hour drive. Aside from occasionally pissing and washing our faces off in Hardee's bathroom sinks, we have just driven eleven hours *straight*. Well, technically we drew straws, and Rich had to drive. I'm not legally allowed to because I don't have my license. "You guys are gonna make me drive the whole way to Tucson?" Rich asks with a pained look in his eyes. "Aww fuck. This is gonna suck so many dicks." That became a popular saying on the tour. "So many dicks." No, it didn't suck just *one* dick. It didn't even suck a few. It sucked *so, so* many. "I have a panic disorder. I can't drive for eleven fucking hours. I'm going to fucking freak out. Make Ronnie do it." Ronnie was a former ambulance driver who somehow got into the "music business" when his legally blind brother-in-law started a touring company out of his house in East Cleveland. They came to my shows, saw an opportunity to make money off my nineteen-year-old back, and signed me to a cross-country touring deal—you know, the dream deal that's brought me to fucking Tucson.

The club looks like a tornado wrecked it forty years ago and nobody bothered to fix it. A warped aluminum sign swings back and forth from a rusted pole, backlit by a dying orange sun with UNCLE PETE'S BAR in faded, hand-painted red, white, and blue. How sad. How American. A forgotten, decrepit little shack on a road with no cars. The only sign that it's still in business is the neon lights that read OPEN in the front window. I can smell cigarette smoke as we step out of the van. Then the smell of poison. A skinny middle-aged man is burning clothes in a *plastic* container out back, thick, billowing black smoke rising from the pile. "He's burning plastic," Timmy whispers in my ear, as if I can't already smell the shit. The man turns slowly and sucks on his Marlboro, eyeing us from under the rim of a Stetson. I imagine he doesn't take too kindly to my long hair or my eyeliner or my jeans so tight that you can see my penis.

"This is gonna suuuuuccccck,"

Rich says under his breath. He's carrying his guitar. He carries it everywhere. Never leaves it in the van. I don't blame him because it was almost stolen twice already, and he pawned off every other piece of musical equipment that he owned to have enough money to go on this tour. It's all he has left. I put on my best optimistic face and turn to Ronnie, who's struggling to breathe in the Arizona heat. Ronnie walks with a limp and is at least a hundred pounds overweight. His rattail bobs up and down behind his head as he struggles to keep up with me. "Ronnie, this is gonna be the best show of the tour. I can feel it," I tell him. He nods and fake smiles back at me. His hands are full of tickets and flyers, which he will sell from a little plastic folding table at the front of the bar. Ronnie's company was supposed to promote the shit out of this tour, using all of their "connections" and their "outstanding reputation in the music business," but every night we find ourselves in a near-empty shithole, playing music for only ourselves, losing money and weight like the poor suckers we are.

We push open the door and enter the bar, expecting to get hit with a blast of air conditioning, but instead we are met with a heat wave even worse than outside. Musty air too thick to breathe. Years of carbon monoxide and beer stuck to every surface. A robust woman in a yellowed T-shirt that says FUCK YOU stares at us from across the dark room. A mop in one hand, a Miller High Life in the other. "You the band?" she asks through twisted teeth that resemble broken tombstones in a forgotten graveyard. "Yes, ma'am. We're Nicholas Megalis," I reply, with a Midwest smile on my face, trying my damnedest to get her to like me. "Who?" "Oh, we're Nicholas Megalis, the headliner," I tell her. She stares at us, unblinking, genuinely baffled. "All four of y'all are Nicholas Bagalis?" she barks. "I am. I'm Nicholas Megalis," I say. "Why'd you say y'all are Nicholas Bagalis then?" she asks, still confused. "No, the . . . the name of the band is Nicholas Megalis. But it's also my name. It's my name and the . . . it's my name and the name of the band also." She stares, shakes her head, and starts mopping the sticky floor. "The stage is over there. Set your shit up," she says, looking down at the floor.

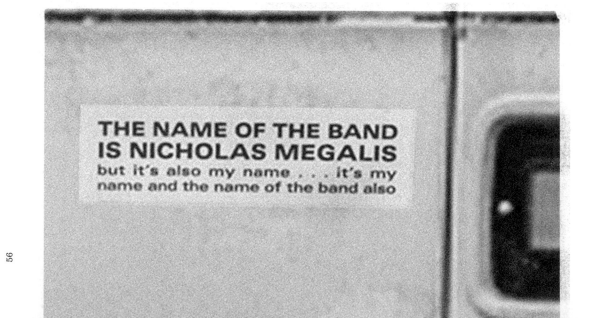

THE NAME OF THE BAND
IS NICHOLAS MEGALIS
but it's also my name . . . it's my
name and the name of the band also

The "stage" is more or less a long box that's only about a foot off the ground. The usual components of a music stage aren't there. No monitors, no speakers, no drum rug, no mic stands, no nothing. Just plywood painted black and an unplugged box fan. I look over at Rich, and he's defeated. He was right. This is absolutely, positively going to suck so many dicks. The fire-exit door swings open, and the skinny guy we saw outside steps into the room. The smell of poisonous smoke wafts in behind him. He reaches into his ass pocket and pulls out a crumpled-up piece of paper. "This here says there are ten bands playing tonight. How the fuck is that gonna happen?" he asks, madder than a striped snake. Ronnie steps forward and takes authority. "Sir, I'm Ronnie, the Nicholas Megalis tour manager. You see, there are ten bands playing *total*, with Nicholas headlining." The guy reaches into his other pocket, pulls out a pack of cigarettes, and lights one up.

"*Headlining*?" he says back in a thick Arizona tongue. "What are you guys, fucking Bon Jovi?" He laughs and looks back at the woman who's mopping, and she laughs too. At this point, I feel like an idiot. This guy has just taken a verbal shit all over us. Bon Jovi. Wow.

"Nicholas will play in between all of the locals so that he can have a crowd, but he's headlining. We have a banner we need to hang up, so can somebody assist me with a ladder?" Ronnie asks with a nervous gulp. The man glares at Ronnie so hard you'd think he woulda popped a blood vessel. "Ain't nobody hanging up a sign in this fucking place. That wall is just painted. Set up your shit," he says, shutting us down completely. Ronnie nods and heads for the exit. I join him outside, leaving my bandmates behind. "Ronnie, it's okay. We don't need to hang up my banner tonight. Let's just play the show and get the fuck out of Tucson."

The sun goes down, but the heat burns on. A tumbleweed rolls by as we all sit outside, waiting on a crowd that will never show. By the way, in case you didn't catch that, I said a fucking *tumbleweed* rolled by. Like the kind in the cartoons. What's next, a scorpion? A rattlesnake with a cowboy hat on? A coyote dropping an anvil on a road-runner? The orange glow slowly disappears over the horizon as the boys and I stare out into the desert. It seems to go on forever and ever. The landscape is dotted with cacti. I point out a cactus that looks like a tall man with a huge erection. Timmy points out one that looks like a tall man with *two* erections. A double-penised man. Ronnie sits at a long plastic table, piled high with T-shirts and posters with my face on them. My balls are sweating so profusely that they stick to my legs like suction cups. Rich buries his face in his hands, cooling off and pretending he isn't here. Timmy drifts in and out of consciousness. It's almost impossible to stay fully awake in this heat. Ronnie checks his watch. "Eight-thirty. You guys are on in fifteen," he says. "But Ronnie, nobody came. Almost every band canceled on us, and there's nobody in there. It's the bartender and the old man. That's it," I protest. "Surely we can push it a little until someone comes. Didn't you guys promote this show?" "Of course we did. We have a great reputation here, Nicholas. This is one of our biggest markets," he says, lying to my face. His company is bogus, and he's bogus, and this whole tour is bogus. A colossal waste of time and money that will eventually come back to bite me in the ass.

Bored out of my mind, and watching a real-live scorpion copulate with another real-live scorpion in the hot sand, I'm starting to wonder why I became a musician in the first place. Soul-crushing disappointment starts to set in like it does every night. What did I expect to gain from this shitty tour? It certainly wasn't fame, because nobody is showing up. And money? We're losing it by the second. My mom calls my cellphone and checks in on me, as she does every few hours on this tour. She's worried beyond words. "Nick, are you eating enough? Are they feeding you guys? Do you need me to give you money?" she asks, half-crying. "I'm fine. I just ate a big meal," I say, lying my ass off. The reality is, I ate a Twix and some beef jerky and washed it down with a three-day-old bottle of stale water that someone threw at my head while onstage in Colorado. "Nick, don't smoke anything or drink anything or eat any pills. You could die! So many rock stars die!" she says, ridiculously implying that I'm a *star*. "Mom, I'm not a rock star. I'm a Greek kid who plays piano. And nobody is coming to these stupid shows," I say, lowering my voice. "These shows have been duds. And whenever we actually have more than three people in the crowd, they're there to see another band, and they throw shit at us, Mom. It's terrible. I hate it." I had to tell her the truth. It's therapeutic. My mom listens well. And she's my mama bird. My caretaker. I drank milk from her boobs. Okay, that got weird. . . .

The old guy comes out the front door and points to the stage. He doesn't even say anything, he just points and stares at us like a serial killer. It's show time. I slap Rich on the back, and he shakes out of his heat coma. The three of us leave Ronnie at the merch table and walk the length of the bar to the foot-high platform where we'll be playing songs for absolutely *nobody*. Our full drum kit, electric guitars and amplifiers, and eighty-eight-key digital piano were set up for no reason whatsoever. It's the worst feeling in the world. But like the budding young professionals that we are supposed to be, Rich straps on his guitar, Timmy sits at the drum kit, and I turn on my keyboard. "Hello," I speak into the mic as it squeals in feedback. There's nobody there to fix the microphone, so I deal with it. The fat lady stands in the back, watching *Judge Judy* on a little black-and-white TV that's mounted above the bar. The old guy stares at us for a second and then walks out to smoke a cigarette.

This might be the lowest moment in my music career. I think of my parents and my siblings, who are all back in Ohio. I think of my friends who are enrolled in college, making their families proud as they train to become functional members of society. I have failed, and I have failed hard. I am standing center stage, one foot off the ground, looking out at an empty little room, and I count the boys off. "1, 2, 3, 4 . . ." Timmy swings into the drums like a butcher might swing at a beef flank. His thin, muscular

AGE 6, PLAYING TO AN ACTUAL AUDIENCE.

IN A LIVING ROOM.

arms create sounds too big to come from just a drum kit. It's like cannons going off in Gettysburg. Rich is machinelike in the glassy light. He strums sexually on his electric guitar, producing a crackling hum that makes me want to weep. But there's no time to weep. I open my mouth and sing loudly into the microphone. My voice echoes out endlessly into the empty room. "Baby, where'd you get your eyes?" my throat booms. It is in this exact moment that I remember why I play music. This moment right here is the *reason* I play music. This feeling. The feeling of control. The feeling of total rock 'n' roll domination. Sweeping over every inch of my physical being. Making me quiver. I can't say I've done hard drugs, but I can tell you that it's probably a similar rush.

In a flash, the show is over. The thrill is gone. And the three of us are packing our gear back into the van. Ronnie walks over to me with a very familiar look on his mug. The look of a man who's about to deliver disappointing news. "Look, guys. There wasn't anyone in attendance tonight, and the bar lost money, so . . ." He hands me an envelope, and I open it. "What are these? Are these . . . no . . . it can't be," I say, examining the contents. "These are fucking coupons. Coupons for Hardee's."

Yes, the bar paid us in roast beef sandwiches. The same sandwiches that fucked our stomachs from Ohio to Arizona. The same indigestible crap that would back my intestines up for days and result in volcanic diarrhea in some truck-stop bathroom. It was garbage food, and it was a big F-you to my band. They could have said, "Look, guys, nobody came. We lost money. Here's some beer. Have a good rest of the tour." But they chose to hand us passports to the worst meals of our lives. The bottom of the barrel. The food of the desperate. Chum bucket–level nastiness on an onion bun. Those bastards.

"At least we played a kick-ass set," Timmy says. His positive outlook in the middle of that broke-down, soul-sucking moment is the tiny flicker of light that I need to lift my spirits. I smile and enter the van for the three millionth time that tour, climbing over mounds of dirty clothing and unsold CDs. Rich sits in the backseat, his face lit only by the screen of his iPod. I can hear the subtle bumps of jazz coming through his earbuds. Ronnie gets into the driver's seat and closes the door behind him, letting out a long sigh of relief. "Fuck Tucson," he says, staring ahead. We all laugh a little, except for Rich, who's lost in his jazz. Ronnie turns the key to the ignition. He turns it again. And once more. And then again. And then once again. And nothing. The van is dead.

And somebody just farted.

PSYCHOTIC Magic OBSESSIONS

I was born with a top hat on my head.

I guess I've always been a performer. Standing naked in the kitchen of our first house, with a deck of cards bigger than my face, faking sleight of hand. Too young to learn, and no attention span. Throwing the cards up in the air as if a trick had just happened. My face, stone cold with resolute intensity. You know the look. All magicians have that face. That's what magic was to me. I didn't understand that there was a science to mastering an illusion. I didn't know that these caped idiots had spent their entire lives crafting their tricks. I didn't give a shit. It was all about the show. The *idea* that something had just happened.

Dazzling people was my first love. Getting attention. It didn't matter what it was for. It could have been juggling, but it was too difficult to learn. My down-the-street neighbor Alex McDougal was a juggler for a bit. His juggling career ended abruptly when he thought he could make the switch from softballs to forks and one landed in his eye. I wasn't too coordinated, and I also didn't enjoy practicing things that didn't come naturally to me. Just inherent laziness, I guess.

I was maybe six or seven years old. I can't exactly pinpoint the first event that sparked my love of magic, but I can name the guy who struck the match: David Copperfield. The raven-haired, John Stamos–looking god of the Vegas strip. I would beg my mom to let me stay up another hour to catch his over-the-top Sunday-night TV special, which I would also record onto not one, but two VHS tapes. One for watching, one for safekeeping under my bed. I would wear a plastic top hat from one of those ten-dollar magic kits you find at the toy store and sit, unblinking, in front of the TV while David did his thing. I wasn't watching the magic tricks as much as I was watching his magic hips. He would hold his assistant by the throat and gently whisper into her ear while a big fan blew their hair back. It was sensual; it was bizarre. I didn't know what the hell was going on. But I watched, and I made mental notes. And I could feel myself slowly transforming into a mini Copperfield, complete with my own out-of-control ego and homemade, horrible magic tricks.

Three or four days into my psychotic magic obsession and my dad has already scored us two tickets to see David on his North American tour. Dad is the enabler, the coddler. Anything I want, he supplies. With no hesitation. He endlessly supports all of my fads and interests, while my mom stands with her arms crossed in protest. "You just spent 150 bucks on nosebleed seats? He's not going to care in a week," Mom scolds my old man. "Look, Denise. Nicky could be the next big magic star. This is his school!" Dad barks back as he buckles me into the Ford Explorer.

The show is spectacular. The ceaseless pyrotechnics and confetti. Constant standing ovations for everything. A big-breasted assistant handing the superhero-esque Copperfield his gigantic table saw, the weapon he would use to split her into two slutty pieces. Spooky music, lots of flashing lights and fog machines. David rolls his sleeves up and interacts with the crowd. He brings a full-grown man in the front row to tears as he guesses his childhood hero. Some fake snow falls, and then Copperfield makes everybody cry with a story about his own childhood. I watch the action on a giant video monitor because my dad was too Greek to get us better seats. Copperfield is in top form tonight. At one point, he literally rides a fucking lion across the stage. Retrospectively, I wonder how long it took to break the lion's spirit enough for him to let that idiot ride him.

The big grand finale is finally here. David's exhausted Mexican stagehands push out a giant box fan. I immediately recognize the trick from his TV special. You know, the one I had recorded, watched, and rewatched maybe 380 times until I figured out exactly how he did the trick. Now, this is pre-Google. I wasn't able to look this crap up on the computer. I studied that VHS tape and figured his sneaky ass out. Copperfield is lowered into a huge industrial-sized fan and apparently ripped to shreds. His bones are too hard to cut through, so the fan "malfunctions." A puff of smoke, and David is gone from the fan, and a spotlight shines on the back of the theater, where David miraculously appears in one of the seats. It's a good trick, but I knew how he did it. I am a magic nerd, and I know how it's done.

Like any kid who doesn't know how to behave in public, I jump out of my seat when David appears in the back of the theater, and I scream out, "That wasn't him!!! That wasn't him!!! That was a body double!!!" My dad nervously covers my mouth and pushes my head down into the seat. He's laughing, but you can tell he's humiliated to be the father of the boy who has ruined the show for everyone. I don't know why I blurted it out. I probably was just jacked on root beer and candy and totally excited that I knew something no one else did.

Magic consumes my life. I stand in line for what seems like days to get a glimpse of Houdini's rusted handcuffs at a traveling magic exhibit in Pittsburgh. My dad invests hundreds of dollars in intricate little illusions that I'll never take the time to learn. I blow through every book ever written on the subject of magic and performance at our local library. I don't know how much I'm even reading. I'm just looking at the black-and-white photos of these tuxedoed madmen posing in front of their elaborate props. And I'm itching to make something of my own. **I NEED A GUILLOTINE.** I ask my dad to make me one. He thinks about it for a second, maybe even sketches one up. And then it dawns on him that it would be life in jail if he ever beheaded his son. My Yia Yia, devoted grandma and seamstress, takes my measurements and crafts a little suit for me with my own initials on the breast pocket. My dad tracks down a milliner in the yellow pages, and he has a real top hat made for me. I look just like the guys in the book, except I'm eight years old and I have a bowl cut and four missing teeth.

One afternoon, my drunk uncle pulls up in his flatbed and drops off a big storage bin in the front yard for my mom to store old baby clothes in. I intercept the delivery and use it for my own weird childhood needs. The bin first functions as a swimming pool, and then as a plastic sex den for my two cats to mate, and then it finally becomes my first magic prop. This will be my escape trick. Like Houdini. If I had read those books more carefully, I would know that Houdini was a genius escape artist and had devoted countless hours to picking locks and meditation. He could hold his breath for twenty minutes, and he could open any handcuffs on the planet. I am eight years old, with the attention span of a gnat, hunched over a stack of newspaper, ripping it into shreds to make confetti. I am already working on the end of a trick that I have no idea how to do. My dad and I practice a trick that I make up on the spot. He blindfolds me, lays me into a blanket, wraps me up, and then lowers my body into the plastic bin, which he "locks" with a loose latch on the back that can easily be popped off with a little nudge from the inside.

It is the premiere of my first show. My mom's dad is coming over to celebrate his fifty-fifth birthday at our house, and it's a perfect evening to debut my death-defying feat. The theater is our living room. The stage is a bedsheet strung over the backs of two kitchen chairs and secured with rubber bands. Backstage, I have a garbage bag filled with the ripped-up newspapers, a boom box loaded with a Depeche Mode cassette, and the plastic bin. My dad, who is in on the trick, is seated in the audience next to my grandparents. My grandfather is already complaining about having to watch the show. And I know this for a fact because there's a videotape somewhere that my mom took, and you can hear his grumpy Pittsburgh voice mumbling under his breath, "Do we have to watch this damn thing?"

My little sister, who is barely four years old, is standing in her overalls on top of the left couch arm, flicking the light on and off with a fly swatter because she's too short to reach the switch. She's the best lighting technician in town. Nobody flicks a light switch like this one. I give her the signal from over the bedsheet to keep the lights on, and I roll out from underneath the sheet. My hat gets caught on the fabric and pulls the entire stage down. My dad quickly jumps out of his chair and fixes the stage while I throw handfuls of newspaper at my grandfather's face to distract him from the malfunction. I'm almost certain that this enrages him, but my grandmother probably pinched his leg, and he forces a smile. Depeche Mode's *Violator* kicks on, and it's time for my dad to bring out the prop. "Your own. Personal. Jesus" blasts out of the tiny speakers, filling the living room with gay European goth dance music. I skip around with an incredibly stern and focused look on my face, while my dad raises the blindfold to put over my gigantic head. My deeply religious grandparents watch as my tiny sister hops down from the arm of the couch, pigtails bouncing, and heads for the bag of confetti. She knows her mark. She's a pro.

My dad rolls me up like a human marijuana joint and gently lowers me into the plastic tomb. I have just seconds to break free from the wrap and pop out of the bin just in time to hit my music cue. Dave Gahan opens his lips to say, "Reach out and touch faith," and that's the moment I emerge. Unharmed! Miraculously! How did I survive being gently secured in a plastic bin for a whole thirteen seconds!? Deeply satisfied, I grin at my audience of unmoved family members, who aren't sure why or when to clap. My sister douses me and the crowd in an explosion of newspaper shreds. And the show is over. My grandfather stands up before anyone else, pats me on the head in disgusted approval, and excuses himself to use the bathroom. My Aunt Debbie pretends that she wants to know how the trick is done and grills me at the end of the show. I repeat that old magic mantra—"A good magician never reveals his secrets"—and she gives me a piece of birthday cake to shut me up. **What a little shit.**

IF A MONKEY WAS TAUGHT HOW TO USE A PEN

The paint markers look extra gorgeous today.

They're glistening in the fluorescent overhead lights of Walmart. I lean in for a sniff. Fresh, toxic plastic. Delicious. I uncap the Robin's Egg Blue and inhale the paint. No, I'm not trying to get high. I'm not that stupid. I am simply in love with the smell of fresh art supplies. And it doesn't stop at markers. A brand new pink eraser can send me into a frenzy. Pull a fresh pencil out of a sharpener and put that sucker up to my nose—I'll die. Yellow legal pads smell like brown sugar. Good God.

I'm thirteen years old and newly obsessed with a certain illegal activity known as graffiti. The act of writing shit on other people's shit. The second most popular crime among bored suburban teenagers after petty theft. Maybe it's the bright colors. Maybe it's the criminality. I don't know. But whatever it is, there's something intoxicating about running from a mall cop after spray-painting a fat penis and balls on the back of a security truck.

"You're going to get arrested, Nick. It's going to happen. Maybe not today, maybe not tomorrow . . . but someday you will pay for this crap," my dad warns me as we stand in the marker aisle. He tells my mom I'm using them on paper so she doesn't slit his throat. "Graffiti is obnoxious, and it's *illegal*," he says with a new intensity as he realizes how much trouble *he* could be in. My dad knows very well that a thirteen-year-old kid won't be paying the fines. It's his money that the city will siphon. "This is a nice neighborhood, Nick. The guy whose garage you drew on yesterday? He's seventy-eight years old. His wife just died. You want him scrubbing that crap?" "Dad, come on. This is my art. This is what I am. I'm a graffiti artist," I say, grabbing a paint marker from the shelf. "And they'll never catch me."

Seven years later. August. I somehow find myself living in the graffiti mecca of the goddamn world. New York City. It's a dream come to fruition. More walls than I know what to do with. The most vandalism I've ever seen in one place. Layer upon grimy layer of SHITFUCK, DONNY27, EDGE, VAPERFUCKER, FUCKTITS.

IF YOU HAVE A CLEAN STOREFRONT, ENJOY IT FOR THE HOUR THAT IT'S CLEAN

Some kid in a hoodie is waiting in the shadows to cover it in spray paint. I'm a lazy twenty-year-old who wants to be a million different things at once. I'm a struggling musician who doesn't have a job and didn't go to college. My obsessions change more often than my clothes. Some days I wake up and decide to be an experimental filmmaker. Other mornings I am a drunken poet.

"Nick, you got paint on our new couch. It's all over the damn cushions. This is ridiculous," my girlfriend says, using her fingernail to scratch away at the drips on our brand new couch, which *she* purchased. "Last night, I painted one of my Spaz faces on a food truck! It was dope!" I tell her excitedly. She's not in the mood for my shit. "Yeah, well, you're going to get arrested. And you owe me $300 for the couch." I don't blame her for being upset. Let's be real—I'm a loser. This whole rebellious, punk-rock lifestyle is cool for eleven minutes. The rest of the time it's just flat-out depressing.

It's Tuesday. I'm playing guitar tonight at the worst club in the city—a dive in the West Village known for its perpetually plugged toilets and a sound system that sounds like it's inside a toilet. This is an attempt to get back into my groove. I've been so distracted since I moved here. Can you blame me? If you don't have a clear focus, you can disappear in New York's insanity. I've gained weight, lost confidence, and have erased all of my songs from my memory with marijuana. "You gotta bring your own stool," the voice on the other end of the phone tells me. I'm on a call with the club, working out last-minute kinks with the unhappiest woman I've ever spoken to. Her voice sounds like two rocks being rubbed together. "To sit on?" I ask, confused. "Yeah, to sit on. We don't have any extra stools." Usually I would just grab one of the many unused chairs from the club, and there are always plenty, because no one comes to my shows. But this woman is telling me that I have to provide my own place to sit. We're off to a great start.

So I play the show. Sing my little Greek heart out. Nobody shows. I told a few friends, but they have lives, and they can hear me sing for free in my apartment. The lady I talked to on the phone gives me a slice of cold pizza and a Cherry Coke as payment. Her long, matted blonde hair and smoke-stained teeth deplete any trace of appetite I had. I sit all lonely at the bar and chew the rubbery pizza very slowly as she complains about Hispanic people and money troubles and her husband's colon disease and whatever else she can dump on me. "The graffiti too. Those motherfuckers. Just got new windows for the bar. But those motherfuckers don't give a shit. They're cocksuckers," she rants. I try not to look directly into her eyes. I don't want her to see my guilt. "Those cocksuckers gotta pay for these windows 'cause I sure as hell ain't paying for it." She slides me a shot of some unknown liquor and pours herself the same. "Cheers . . . cocksuckers."

The Night is Young

I have a little pep in my step. I ended up drinking four or five shots of free booze with the gravelly-voice lady, and I almost cried in front of her at one point. I'm on my feet now, almost dancing as I move about the street. I dip into another bar, buzzed and feeling fancy. A big bulldog-looking guy is sitting in a chair inside the front entrance. He puts his arm out to stop me. "ID," he says in a voice too deep to be real. Almost sounds like he's speaking whale. I pull out my wallet with supreme drunken confidence and hand him my fake. He inspects it with a flashlight and looks up at me, looks back down, then up at me, then back down, and hands it back. "Have a good night," he says, glaring. I think he knows it fake, but he's not in the mood to toss me on my ass. My lucky night.

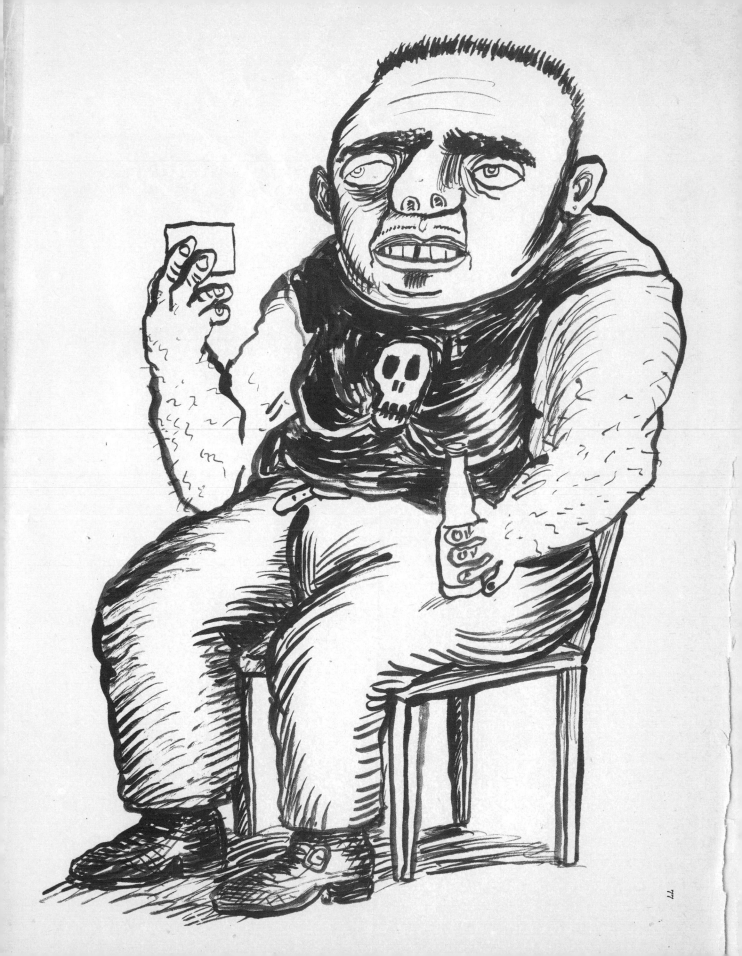

See, the problem with me is one drink is never enough. I can't have just *a* shot. One beer is stupid; don't even try to give me just *one* beer. Alcohol awakens something inside of me that I can't contain. It's a beast waiting to explode from my chest like in those *Alien* movies. What a fucking maniac. But it's not just alcohol. I love chocolate cake too. I have an insatiable appetite for *everything*. It's been this way since I was a fetus. The doctor said I consumed so much nourishment from my mother that I actually took a dump inside the womb, and the nurses had to suction it out of my mom after I was born. With a big vacuum hose. Gross.

After spending every last dime I have to my name, I'm jacked on liquid courage and ready to bounce out of there. Smiling and singing the Beastie Boys' "Skills to Pay the Bills" at full volume with all the wrong lyrics, I exit the bar and trip on a crack in the cement. I land flat on my face in someone's condom wrapper, but I'm okay. A guy passing by on a bike laughs at me, and I try to flip him the bird, but I can't even manage that. I'm not obliterated, but I'm definitely drunk. Too drunk to make responsible adult decisions, at least. I swing my heavy guitar case around as I lift myself off the ground. I wish I played harmonica. The buildings all seem to vibrate when you're this intoxicated. The street liquefies a bit underneath your shoes, and walking becomes a daunting task. Voices echo out of everywhere. Sirens whirl around your little head. The sky is closer to the ground than ever before. I can almost grab the stars. "Fruck yoo!" an Asian guy screams at an old white woman with saggy tits. I laugh, swinging my guitar case. Life isn't real in New York City. It's a pulsating orb of constantly rotating strangeness unlike any other spot on the planet.

Oh, yeah, I forgot I have a marker.

I feel around in my pants pocket. It's a fat one. A super-duper Sharpie. I pull it out and uncap it for a quick whiff. Memories of my childhood float through my nasal passages. My mother giving me stacks of computer paper to draw on. Sitting on the patio drawing

little faces for hours and hours in the summer heat. The box of markers, never-ending, perpetually being replenished by my wonderful mom. God is good, and God is an artist. I am so drunk. I can smell dog shit, but it almost smells delicious, something sweet and nutty about it. A gay club throbs with bass all down the street. I add my own words over the muffled beat. "I'm a little drunk boy. I'm a drunk boy," I talk-sing against the techno. I can hear a car crash down the block.

A baby is crying. But it's too late for a baby to be awake. I glance to my left and it's actually a full-grown woman. I laugh. With one hand on the handle of my guitar case and one hand holding a marker, I skip-hop down the subway stairs to catch my train back to Brooklyn. I shall continue this night of inebriated bliss in the comfort of my own apartment. I have a six-pack in the fridge and a DVD of *The X-Files* calling my name. I whistle something unknown but familiar. It's a melody I always whistle when I'm in this place of relaxation and joy. It almost could be a pirate song. I could be wasted at sea, with just me guitar and me whiskey to pass the time. I can almost feel the waves swelling and crashing, my ship dipping up and down in God's mighty palm. I swipe my MetroCard a few times, too trashed to get it right on the first try. On the platform, it's just me. Standing, sweating, waiting for my Brooklyn-bound R train in the flickering fluorescent lights. I set my guitar down, uncap my fat-tipped Sharpie once more, and take a whiff. I can almost smell my mom's peanut butter cookies. I can hear my dog barking as I practice my graffiti lettering and eat cookies on the patio. Life is beautiful. I miss my mom. I should call her when I get home. No, I'm too drunk. Tomorrow.

MY ARM IS NOT UNDER MY MIND'S CONTROL.

My mind is wandering someplace else. I push the marker to the glossy surface of a poster advertising some new organic toothpaste. The shit they sell. I draw a face so small, you can barely see it with the naked eye. I draw it right inside the tooth of the smiling lady on the poster. All pearly whites, except for one tooth with a Nicholas Megalis original. "Excuse me." I can hear a voice but no one's here. "Excuse me, sir." Maybe I'm imagining things. I am pretty sauced, after all. I turn with a wobbly head, my eyes half-adjusted, and notice a stocky little guy approaching me. He's wearing a polo, with two wet sweat spots right under his nipples. He's got shorts on and thick, meaty legs. His head disappears into his shoulders, leaving little room for a neck, his buzzed hair dewy with sweat. He's now about a foot from me, and he comes up to my shoulders. "Did you just draw on that poster?" he asks in a friendly but direct tone. "Yes, I did," I answer. He reaches behind his back and pulls out a pair of handcuffs with one hand and lifts his polo up to reveal a badge clipped to his shorts pocket. "Do you have any weapons or sharp objects on you? Anything that will hurt me?" he asks, still friendly, as he routinely and gently moves my arm closer to my other arm to cuff me. "N . . . no," I say, adjusting to what's happening. He holds my arms together with one hand, and with his other, he pats down my legs and butt and pants pockets. "Okay, sir, you are under arrest." It must be a joke. A hidden camera prank. This is New York City. This kind of shit happens all the time. Someone is filming a prank show, and I'm the victim. I look around for the cameras, and nothing. Wait, here comes another guy. Another stocky guy with the same haircut and a different color polo.

"We got one," the first guy says to his approaching buddy. So wait, these guys are cops? They aren't even dressed like cops! What the fuck

is going on? They slap high fives. "Nice catch, Alvarez," says the second guy to my arresting officer. He looks down at my guitar case. "What's in this?" he asks me. I am straddling the edge of tears, my mouth quivering as I try to push the words up from my nauseous stomach. "It's, it's my . . . my guitar, sir," I stammer. He opens the case, and lo and behold it's a fucking guitar. "Nice," he says, as he closes it back up and lifts it to carry with him. We start to walk away, and I look back and see my uncapped Sharpie drying out next to its lid in a crack on the subway platform. Left to die. Like the dream I had of being a famous graffiti artist. "So why did you do that?" my arresting officer asks me as the three of us make our way up the stairway that I had just drunkenly skipped down not even ten minutes ago.

"I'm an artist, sir," I choke. "You think that's art? Ruining people's shit?" "No, sir," I choke again. "Yeah, well it ain't."

So begins my first time in the back of a police car. The front windows are rolled down, and the breeze is washing over my face. It feels good. It dries my tears. I'm so fucking scared. I can't even believe this. It's insanity. My parents were right this whole time. I'm a goddamn idiot. What a stupid thing to have happen. Why couldn't I have just gotten a cheeseburger and gone home? Why did I have to bring that stupid fucking Sharpie with me? I'm a singer. I'm not some criminal. The ride is long, sickening. My guts get tossed around as we hug every curb and run every red light. And I thought cab drivers were psychotic. These guys are joyriding through Manhattan like nobody's business while I'm praying to God above that I don't blow chunks.

I close my eyes and pretend I am back home in Ohio. Life was simpler in the 'burbs. My curfew was 10:00 p.m. when I was eighteen years old. And you know what? Thank God. My parents were tough on me for good reason. Look at me now. I'm a fuckup. I slipped. I slipped *hard*. "Excuse me, officer. Am I going to jail?" I manage to ask through my shaking nerves. "Yeah, but you won't be in there long. We gotta take you in, bud." For some reason, I believe him. These guys aren't the evil, crooked cops in the movies. They're reasonable gentlemen doing their reasonable job.

The car pulls up to this big old copper door that looks like something out of *The Wizard of Oz*. It's probably thirty feet tall. Solid steel. The cop riding shotgun steps out of the car and punches a number into a dirty keypad, and the door starts to lift off the ground. Inside, it's another world. Just bizarre. Imagine *Teenage Mutant Ninja Turtles* meets *The Matrix*. Exposed pipes shooting steam, cops huddled around each other grunting and laughing and smoking cigarettes. Fat cops, short cops, tall cops, all cops. We are in the belly of the New York Police Department. "Welcome to Central Booking, kid." This is some Dick Tracy shit. Some cartoony Roger Rabbit shit. The cop who busted me whispers into my ear as they lead me down the hottest hallway on the planet. (No air conditioning + August = God help us.) "Listen, you're gonna be fine," he says, sensing my fear. "Just don't look Jones in the eye. He's the Mexican guy booking you." This marks the first time in my life I've been sincerely warned to not look someone in the eye.

We enter a white room. Well, not quite white. It's covered in yellowed posters from the '70s warning of the growing drug and illegal immigration problems in New York. And the white bricks aren't even white. They're stained with all kinds of shit. Probably actual shit too. It smells like cologne, sweat, and bleach. My shirt is stuck to my skin. The buzz of fluorescent lights. A fat Mexican guy sits at a desk and barks at me like a dog. "Stand against the wall." Oh, my God. This is it. This is my first mug shot. I'm not gonna lie, part of me is excited to take this photo. I feel like Frank Sinatra in his famous mug shot. I want to look ruggedly handsome in this photo so I can use it for an album cover someday, assuming I get out of here alive. "Stand against the wall!" he yells, because I didn't move fast enough. As I place my back along the wall, I accidentally push the cuffs further into my wrists, almost cutting them with the jagged metal. The feeling of being restrained is too much for me. Panic swells up in my stomach and out through my mouth, and I vomit on the floor. "Oh, Jesus! Get this kid a fuckin' garbage can!" the Mexican says with a New York accent, combining two stereotypes into one incredible, exaggerated man.

It's too late. I throw up again, this time onto my shirt and shoes. It drips off my lips like cereal from a baby's mouth at breakfast. I'm humiliated. They snap the photo. *Flash*. The bulb goes off in my face. Just like in the movies. Someone grabs my arms. It's a new set of cops. The guys who brought me in are nowhere to be found. This time it's a huge white guy with a fucking *patch* over one eye. Maybe this *is* a movie. Maybe they cast this horrifying actor and gave him an eye patch. Nah, this is real life. **THIS SHIT IS MY *LIFE* RIGHT NOW. I CAN'T BELIEVE THIS.** I should have stayed home. Why did I even play that stupid show? Wait. Where is my guitar? "Excuse me, where's my guitar?" I ask, with vomit trickling down my lips. The room of misfit cops all stare at me, dead silent. Oh, God. Somebody has my guitar. Did they put it in the trunk when they picked me up? Is it back at the train station? "Does somebody have my guitar?" I ask again. Eyepatch tugs my arm like some alien guard in a sci-fi movie, and off we go. Out the door. Down another hallway that smells like body odor. Past other prisoners. A man with a face completely soaked in blood is being led down the same hallway going the opposite way, and as he passes me, he smiles.

I enter another room. This one has a sort of minimalist approach. A white chair with an actual shit stain on it, literally a brown stain where an ass crack had been. And a desk. Eyepatch mumbles something about sitting down, so I sit down on the shit stain and cringe. I can smell it. The last guy who sat in this chair *shit himself*. The stench rises up through my jeans. It's a strange feeling to smell poop coming from your pants that isn't your own.

Eyepatch opens a drawer and pulls out a piece of paper and a pen, then closes the drawer. He opens his mouth to speak, showing off a set of the gnarliest yellow teeth I've ever seen. It's as if all his teeth were at war with one another, and they all just died. His breath is offensive. Fishy. Stale. "You will write down what you did and all the other stuff you did before tonight. I'm gonna cuff you to this chair. Don't try anything you're gonna regret." Shrek with an eye patch uncuffs my one hand and cuffs it to the chair I'm sitting in. Another reminder that I am a piece of human garbage and this guy is taking out the trash. "Let's go. Quickly," he says, putting the pen in my free hand.

So, I'm supposed to write down all the crimes I've ever committed? "So . . . so you want me to write down any . . . like, any, uh . . . crimes I've . . . crimes I've committed in my . . . *life*?" I ask. He's not pleased with my confusion. He doesn't answer, at all. Not even a nod. I write the first things that come to my head. I'm so damn nervous I don't even know if they're crimes or not. I just start writing. The list kind of looks like the following, except imagine it in the shakiest handwriting you've ever seen. Imagine if a monkey was taught how to use a pen. That's what this looks like.

1. I drew a face on a sign tonight.
2. I drew a face on a sign before.
3. I stole a Lemonade from a gas station.
4. I stole a small pack of Kleenex from Target.

I am now seated in my cell. Except it's not *my* cell. It's a shared cell with maybe twenty of the toughest looking sons of bitches on the planet. A big cage with one long metal bench running against all three walls. Then bars. Big, serious bars. Cold steel.

The biggest prisoner is seated next to a pay phone—a morbidly obese black guy with a shirt that says MONEY FAME FAMILY. His bulbous head looks like a brown balloon blown up beyond a safe size, and he's leaning against the phone, dead asleep. The guy next to him is shaking as he sleeps. Little jolts of energy blast through him every few seconds. I'm not sure if it's a medical condition or drugs or what. Across from him are two short guys in pulled-up red socks. They're speaking Spanish. I understand a few curse words. Everyone's shoes are missing laces. That's because when they throw you in here, they take away the laces so you don't hang yourself or strangle someone else.

There's no place for me to sit. In the back left corner of the cell is a cracked, shit-stained toilet without any doors. If you have to take a dump, you do it in front of everyone. Over the course of the next hour or two, or God knows because I don't have a watch, two guys take horrendous dumps. Then the toilet paper runs out. There's nothing to wipe our asses with, so people start using their hands and smuggled newspapers. Someone clogs the toilet with the newspapers. Then a guy who I'm guessing is

legally blind uses his own foot to push the shit and newspapers down. I'm trapped in a room with this. And Lord, the heat is oppressive. I have to stand against the wall or sit down on the floor, and I keep rotating positions because nobody will give up their seat on the metal bench. One guy is shoeless. His hairy, ashy feet are propped up on another guy's lifeless body. A really skinny guy with no teeth is shouting about the Lord. "You have all sinned. You have all failed Him! That is why you are here! You have sinned! You are sinners, and you have failed the Lord! He will have his day!" the skinny guy yells at us. I'm on the cold floor, my face buried between my knees. I'm secretly crying down here. If anyone sees me cry, won't they kill me? That's what I've heard. I heard people get murdered in jail for being pussies. And I am the biggest pussy I know.

Every once in a while the prison officer, or PO as they say in here, walks past our cell to stop a fight or warn us of the consequences of our actions or remind us that breakfast will be served. When I hear the word *breakfast*, it finally hits me that I've been in here for hours and hours. And my girlfriend is probably about to wake up for work. She will turn to kiss me, and my side of the bed will be vacant. Since my cellphone was taken from me when I was booked, I will have to use the pay phone to tell her I'm in jail. Except there's a gigantic ogre of a man snoring up against it. Drool drips from his mouth onto his open palms, as if he's catching it like rainwater in a third world country. Occasionally, the PO walks by and shouts at someone, and the pay phone sleeper wakes up and curses at him and then drifts back into sleep.

I somehow work up the courage to get off my ass on the cold floor and walk over to the phone. A few guys start to whisper behind my back as I take my first steps. "He's gonna wake up Cubby," they say. "He better not wake Cubby." I'm holding back tears and vomit. I'm not drunk anymore, but I still have a tiny ounce of liquid courage deep in my soul, and I use that last little drop of it to touch the man's gigantic arm. One of his eyes opens up, and then the other eye. "What are you fucking doing?" he asks under his breath, stern and scary, in a deep black-guy voice that I couldn't imitate if I tried. "You fuckin' touching me for?" he says. "I'm sorry. I need . . . I need to use the pay phone." He glares hard at me for a good ten seconds, and the whole room is silent. They're waiting for this guy to smash my face against the ground and knock all my teeth out. But after what seems like an eternity, Cubby moves his shoulder from the pay phone just enough for me to lean in and pick it up. "Thank you so much," I say. He closes his eyes.

This phone takes quarters. I have nothing. Not even lint to roll around between my sweaty fingers.

For a second, there's the sound of an air conditioner unit turning on. Then I realize it's just a power vacuum in the holding cell next to us, and judging by the commotion and smell, it's sucking up someone's puke. I dial Catherine's number. Actually, I fuck up the first two or three times because I can't hold my hand still enough to dial. "Please insert *two* dollars," the automated robot woman says on the other end. I search around frantically for someone friendly-looking enough to borrow a few bucks from, but literally every single man in this room looks like he would rip my face off and eat it. Someone farts in the far corner, and the other dude punches him in the face. Then someone else punches the puncher in the face, and within six seconds, two POs enter the cell, holding everyone back while they cuff two guys and remove them from the cell. Where will they go? Who cares.

"Please insert *two* dollars. Or enter your credit card number followed by the pound sign," the voice reminds me. Shit. Okay, think. . . . I reach around in my pants pockets. Wait, oh, my God. My debit card. My ass pocket. I have it! I actually have it! I always do this when I'm drunk at a bar—I forget to put the card back in my wallet, and I just shove it into a random pocket and hope it's still there in the morning. What a lazy idiot. But being an idiot has saved me today.

"Charging *twenty-five* dollars." Jesus Christ. *Ring. Ring. Ring. Ring. Ring.* "Hello?" Catherine says in a barely audible whisper. "Catherine, it's Nick. I'm in jail. Literally." Silence. Heavy sigh. "Okay, so are you coming home?" "No, I'm in jail, Catherine. I don't know how long I'm here, but I'm going to get breakfast with the guys now and then I'll call you later if I can." Heavy sigh again. "I knew this would happen." Click. She hangs up on me. Wow. My only connection to the outside world has just disconnected.

"Breakfast line. Let's *go!*" the PO shouts from outside our animal cage. He's maybe forty. His face is beat. He's seen some shit, you can tell in his eyes. And he's jaded. We are cattle to him. "Everyone stand in two lines in the cell, and we'll cuff you all together to get your breakfast. Let's fuckin' move, people!" Two more POs, looking even more jaded and pissed off than the first, enter the cage with two long chains, with ten single cuffs on each chain. "Everybody hold out your right arm," the one PO says as the other PO demonstrates. Imagine the stewardesses on a flight showing you how to use your seat as a flotation device except instead of pretty women with southern accents, they're angry, ugly bastards.

This marks the first time I have ever been in a chain gang. Another thing that I thought only took place in old movies. But this shit's *real*. We are all chained together, shuffling along, one after the other, in a line to get lukewarm sandwiches. Not even sandwiches—scratch that. It's two pieces of Wonder Bread with a piece of cheese in the middle or a dollop of peanut butter. And everybody gets milk in the little cartons like back in grade school. "Pick a sandwich," the chick behind the counter yaps at me. Her enormous, drooping tits slap against each other while she leans over to her milk cart to grab a carton. "Is that just peanut butter, or is there jelly?" I ask. "Pick a fucking sandwich!" she screams. "Cheese."

I eat my sandwich on the floor, picking at the pieces that look moldy. The bread is damp. Soggy. And to wash it down, a room-temperature sour milk. We are nothing.

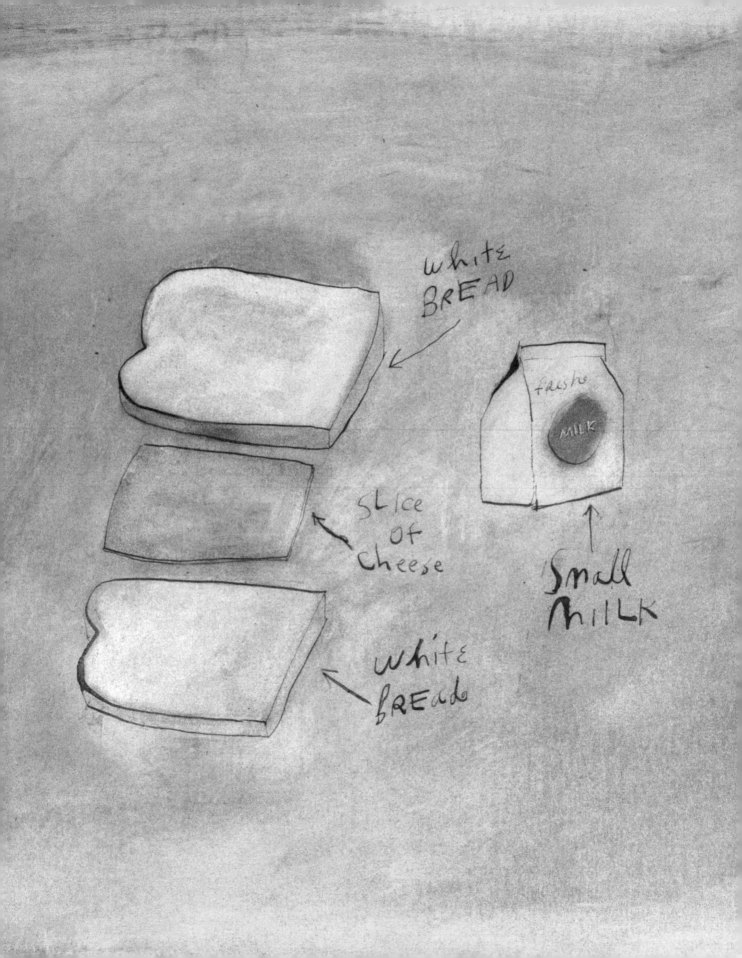

white
BREAD

slice
of
cheese

white
bread

fresh
MILK

Small
MILK

We are garbage. This is why you don't commit crimes, I think to myself. I wanna hammer this into my fucking skull. I want to remember every smell, every tear, every face. I can't come back here. Ever, ever, ever, ever again. "You want my milk?" asks a friendly voice. I look up, and it's a big guy with taped spectacles and a sweaty red face. His button-down shirt is unbuttoned almost the whole way, and his gut is hanging over his work pants. It looks like he was arrested at his software engineering job. He's smiling at me, holding out his unopened milk. "I can't drink it. I'm lactose intolerant." Obviously, I can't possibly drink his milk even if I wanted to. Even if I were in the desert, I couldn't. Because I don't trust him. For all I know, he injected some sort of drug or disease into it. I politely accept the milk and smile back. "What are you in for?" he asks me. "Graffiti. You?" "Cocaine. It was my last straw, though. Probably going away for fifty years. I'll never get to see my son again."

And this is the point where I just about lose my mind completely. I shoot up off the ground and power walk over to the bars and try to poke my head through, just enough to see what's happening peripherally, but I can't see anything. It's designed so that you can't see to the right or left of your cell. That's probably the worst part. The suffocation. The feeling of being trapped and blind to your fate. It's the worst shit ever. I sit back down on the floor, facing the wall, and cry. One of my tears lands on some guy's naked feet, and he calls me a "cracker bitch." Another guy spits a cheese sandwich phlegm ball an inch from my head. I cry silently, but hard.

"Let's fuckin' go! Let's move!" the PO yells into the cage. Is he calling my name? No, this can't be. I wipe my tears away. No, it's too good to be true. "Yes! I'm him. I'm Megalis!" I say, darting up. "It's your hearing. Let's go." It's true. God is real, and he loves me. Thank you, thank you, thank you, thank you, thank you.

"So, you're a guitar player?" the public defender asks me from behind bulletproof glass. She has been appointed as my lawyer because I can't afford one. And she's beautiful. Drop dead gorgeous. Her long red hair perfectly frames her heart-shaped face. Her cheeks are freckled and rosy. Her eyes lock onto mine. "Did you hear me?" I snap out of my trance. Shit. "Yes, sorry. I'm a musician," I say. "I don't do graffiti. This is a fluke. I was coming home from a show, and I got caught by an undercover. I was just drawing on a tooth." "On a tooth?" "Yeah, I was drawing a little face, and this guy caught me and it was a fluke. I don't do graffiti. I write stupid songs. I swear to God." I think she feels bad for me because she basically tells me that she will get me off with no charges as long as I do the following things:

1. Don't Look Judge in the Eye.
2. Don't SAY A Word. Just Nod.
3. Comb my hair.

"If you comb your hair, you won't look so . . . disheveled," she says, kind of laughing but also serious. "Just run your fingers through it. You kind of look like a homeless person. And button your shirt up one more."

I'm standing in a hallway now, next to my public defender, who smells *amazing* by the way. And she's basically telling me "I've got this" without actually saying it. As if the whole thing is rigged and she knows a cheat. Her confidence is so reassuring and uplifting that it rubs off on me, and I enter the courtroom like a champ.

"Nice shirt." What? "I like your shirt, man," a security guard says, not making eye contact with me. He's not even being facetious. He's giving me a genuine compliment. "Thanks, man. She told me to button it up."

"Your honor, this young man is a musician. He was out after a show, and he had a Sharpie, and he was drawing on a sign. It was a mistake, and he has no prior criminal

record. He promises to stay away from graffiti and all other illegal activities and to focus on his career as a recording artist." She glances over at me and gives me a lip-bite that, in turn, gives me a legal boner. She's got this whole courtroom in her little freckly hands. She walks back to me, her high heels clicking against the marble floor. Her perfume is flowery and subtle. Her breath is warm as she whispers, "We've got this."

The judge looks through a stack of papers and then at my defender's ass and then back at the stack of papers, and I'm willing to bet the pages were blank. "Mr. Megalis, I find you responsible and guilty of criminal mischief. You will be put on six months' probation with no additional community service." Then he gets up and leaves. Not even the hammer thing that judges are supposed to do. That's it, I guess.

My public defender is gone too. Just like that. Not even a kiss good-bye. I can smell her on me still. What a creep. I'm such a fucking creep. The guard who complimented my shirt escorts me out of the courtroom and into a hallway and says, "Have a good one, man. Great shirt." And that's really it. I can smell the summer again. It slowly replaces the staleness in my nostrils. I am through the revolving doors and out into the street. No cuffs. No chain gang. No tears. A kid rides past me on a bike, blasting Tupac on a boom box that's duct-taped to the basket. A Chinese lady is selling grapefruit under a tattered umbrella. Two of the most beautiful girls I've ever seen are walking down the street, laughing about something or other. And everyone outside is *free*.

I will retire from graffiti for good today. I wasn't even that good at it, anyway. I will throw away all my spray paint and markers, erase the graffiti image searches in my Internet history, and wave politely to every cop I ever see from this day forward. I might even throw in a "How do you do, officer?" as I cheerfully skip down the street like a good law-abiding citizen of the United States of America. I will live a timid, boring existence, desperately afraid of law enforcement. I will get a real job, pay taxes, and fall asleep at a reasonable time. My hobbies will be gentle and harmless. **And I will never eat another cheese** ★ ★ ★ ★ ★ ★ ★ ★ ★ ★ **sandwich for the rest of my natural life.**

★ ★ ★ ★ ★ ★ ★ ★ ★ ★ ★ ★ ★ ★ ★ ★ ★ ★ ★ ★
★ ★ ★ ★ ★ ★ ★ ★ ★ ★ ★ ★ ★ ★ ★ ★ ★ ★ ★ ★
★ ★ ★ ★ ★ ★ ★ ★ ★ ★ ★ ★ ★ ★ ★ ★ ★ ★ ★ ★

SKIN PILLOWS

I'm peering out above the swaying trees.

I can see all the rooftops in the neighborhood. "Hand me the binoculars, Alec." Alec, my trusty albino lookout is seated behind me with all the supplies. He digs through a book bag and pulls out the binoculars and a pack of smokes. You see, Alec is the head of a local cigarette-thieving ring. He and his business partner, a fat kid named Bullet who has a rattail and horrible breath, will go into a restaurant and locate the cigarette machine. They're usually in the back near the pay phones. Alec will make a scene to the clientele about a "bad bike accident out on Mill Road" while Bullet feeds the cigarette machine five-dollar bills, and then they turn around and sell loose smokes after school. Today, he's kind enough to share the spoils. We chain-smoke like champions. We are like the Marlboro Man's illegitimate children.

Alec is the whitest kid I know. He's an albino. His skin is translucent, and on a sunny day he looks like a dryer sheet. When he holds his hands up to the sun, you can see all of his bones. His eyes are black and beady, and he spits when he talks. He's a natural-born troublemaker, a squirrel mutilator, and he's my personal connection to every single badass in town—a liaison between me and the kids I'm not supposed to hang out with. "You know what a pussy is, right?" he asks me, while I adjust the focus on the binoculars. "Yeah, the Onion gave me, like, a million porno magazines, and I seen a million pussies, just the other day," I proudly exclaim. What I won't tell Alec is that all of the magazines were destroyed by my dad's Ford Explorer, and that the old man who lives in the corner house had to clean up all of the porn with a rake. Like a pile of leaves. Except vaginas.

"So dude, the house I was telling you about is red brick with a white roof. There's a dog in the yard and a guy smoking a cigarette. You see it, dude?" Alec whispers, as if the people we are spying on could hear us from two hundred yards away. We are perched in the treehouse that we built together with our bare hands, trying to get a glimpse of a sixty-year-old woman's breasts. Alec, also the neighborhood pervert, has mapped out all of the houses where you can see women taking their clothes off through the windows. And this particular spot is home to Mrs. Endleson, a retired nurse with gigantic boobs. Alec has seen them before, and he's overjoyed to share the vision with his good friend Nick. That's me, in case you were wondering. I'm Nick.

"I can't see anything, Alec. She's not home," I complain. Alec doesn't answer. He's too busy loading a slingshot. "What the hell are you doing?" I ask him. He pushes me out of the way and draws the sling back as far as it'll stretch, while squinting one beady black eye. In an instant, he releases the rubber band, and the rock flies away from the treehouse and shatters Mrs. Endleson's bedroom window. Their dog is going nuts, barking his furry ass off. Alec pulls the binoculars off of my neck and stares into the direction of the broken window. **"FUCKING JACKPOT!"** he screams. He can barely contain himself. "Let me see, dude!" I demand, grabbing the field glasses from his see-through hands.

There in my scope, two hundred yards away, are Mrs. Endleson's gigantic, varicose milk bags. She's standing in the window, topless and confused, yelling at her husband. Her droopy skin pillows swing back and forth while she inspects the damaged window. While I'm busy getting an eyeful of her thick, salami-sized nipples, my partner in crime is already halfway down the ladder, making a run for it. "I'm going home, Nick! I gotta eat dinner!" he yells back at me without looking. In a flash, the kid is gone. At the time, I assumed he was telling the truth about dinner. But when I think about it as an adult, I can't help but wonder if he was rushing home to do the deed. You know, the deed you do with your right hand in the powder room of your parent's house while they're at the grocery store.

What a brilliant little bastard.

He was a schemer. An albino con man. A pale-skinned Charles Ponzi. Desperate to see skin, no matter how wrinkly and liver-spotted it was, the kid came up with a beautiful little method to summon the titties. He snake-charmed those breasts right up to the window, and all he used was a pebble, a tree branch shaped like a Y, and an old rubber band. Watching him steal, cheat, and be rotten was like watching Pablo Picasso paint a clay pot. He was an artist, a master of bad behavior. And he inspired me that day.

I take one last glance through the binoculars, and the boobies are gone. The party's over. Everybody go home. Mr. Endleson is on his hands and knees on the front lawn, picking up shards of glass with a cigarette hanging out of his mouth. I scan the neighboring houses, but nothing. That's okay. I'm more than ready to head home. With a feeling of horny accomplishment, I turn around and reach for a cigarette from a stolen pack of Camels. I take one out of the pack and light it with a (stolen) pack of matches. I take a deep hit off the cigarette, and then I hear it. The sound of cracking. Ever so quiet. Ever so gentle. Like ice on a pond. I stare down at the wood planks that we crudely wedged between the branches a whole summer ago. They are decayed, weathered, and definitely not suitable for recreational use by human beings. I distinctly remember Alec saying, "Two nails is enough. It's not gonna break." You know, because taking major shortcuts in architecture is always a safe and respectable practice.

Alec was dead wrong, that pale little idiot. The planks give to the weight of my body, and I plummet to the forest floor. A short drop, but a brutal hit. Staring up at the

treetops, I'm breathless. It knocked the wind out of me. I try to call out for help, but I'm incapable. Mute. I can hear birds chirping and a faraway lawnmower, so I know I'm alive. Lying there in the dirt, on God's green earth, I'm wondering if the big man upstairs has finally punished me. I'm petrified that I have done something morally wrong by spying on that poor woman's massive mammaries. I'm questioning my purpose on this planet, wondering if I might have finally broke the camel's back . . . wondering if I'm going to hell. I close my eyes and say a prayer out loud. "Thank you, God, for saving my life. I promise to do good things. I'm never going to do that again. I'm sorry. Amen."

I cross myself,

get up,

brush off the leaves,

and head home

to play with myself.

MY MOTHER MUHAMMAD ALI

School absolutely, positively, undoubtedly, undeniably *sucks*.

I don't care who you are, where you're from, or if you agree with me or not. School is a nightmare for every child on this planet, and that's the goddamn truth.

My deeply fervent hatred for school began the very second my mom Sharpied my name onto my tiny little idiot book bag. It looked like a book bag made for a chihuahua. Mini-sized, because what the fuck do preschoolers need to carry around? I picked it out myself at Kmart, according to my mother. "You liked it because it had Spider-Man on it," she tells me.

Spider-Man wasn't enough to make me like school. In fact, if anything, Spidey was an asshole for tricking me into wearing this book bag, and I hated him now too. That web-slinging liar. Making school look fun, swinging from building to building and whatnot.

I sit at the kitchen table, staring down into my pancakes. My mother is an expert pancake maker. She could knock Julia Child on her *ass*. Mom's pancakes are just too

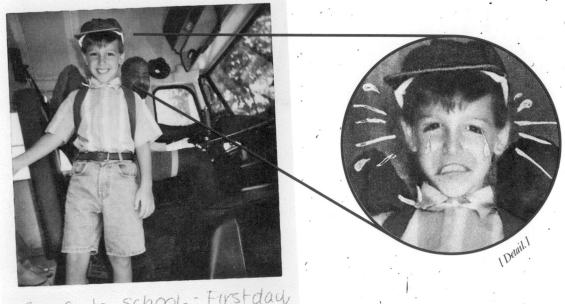

Going to school - First day
Sept '94 Nicholas 5yrs

[*Detail.*]

good to exist. Fat, buttery slabs of doughy delight, lightly crispy on the edges and soft inside. But today, I'm far from hungry. I can't get my hand to move the fork into my mouth. "A dream you dream alone is a dream. But a dream you dream together is a reality," Mr. Rogers says, quoting the late John Lennon on our tiny black-and-white TV. Shut up, Mr. Rogers. Shut your idiot mouth.

We arrive at St. Patrick's, and I blow chunks. *Exorcist* style. Somehow, from the backseat, the vomit still manages to hit the dashboard. Bits of orange juice–soaked pancake drip down from the cassette player. We park the car, my mom unbuckles me from my car seat, cleans me up, rubs my head, and gives me a long hug. "I'll be there with you the whole day. Even when I'm not there. Just think of me and I'm *there*," she promises me, staring into my tear-filled eyes. What a crock of shit.

Quick. I need a plan. I can't go in there and meet my executioner. I go limp. I collapse and fall to the ground. My poor mom tries to lift my tiny body up, but I'm impossibly floppy. Instead of reasoning with an insane child, like some parents would, my mom proceeds to drag my lifeless corpse by my book bag straps through the entire length of the parking lot as I squeal like a pig in a PETA slaughterhouse video.

"PLEASE, GOD! PLEASE!!!!"

I plead at the top of my lungs as we arrive at the school entrance. An older lady in a hideous brown blouse stands in the doorway with her jaw clenched, trying her best to keep a smile as she greets the new students and their parents. She clearly hates people.

"And who might this be?" the brown blouse lady asks as she leans in to inspect me. My mom pinches the back of my neck and I tell her, "Nicholas." She fakes a toothy yellow smile and gives me a look with her eyes that I can only describe as "pure evil." I know that under her human face is a demon face, and under her jet-black dyed hair, a set of horns. I remember the smell of her perfume. It almost smelled like farts. Retrospectively, I realize that it was probably because she was just farting.

This lady turns out to be the principal. Fantastic. They put someone who is clearly the Dark Prince dressed in someone else's skin *in charge* . . . of the *entire school*. She's running the show with her scaly hands. She's the puppeteer, and the preschoolers are her puppets. My mom leans in and whispers into my ear. I don't remember what she says, but I imagine it was something along the lines of, "We'll have pizza for dinner if you go in there."

Just then, the Devil takes me by the hand and leads me away from my mother. Her palm is hot to the touch because, you know, she lives in hell. Mom waves good-bye as I quietly sob. We turn the corner, and her beautiful face vanishes like a dream. "Welcome to Saint Patrick's, Nicholas!" says a very tall woman standing next to a very short lady. "We're your teachers. I'm Ms. Pat," the short one says. "And I'm Ms. Patty," the Amazon chimes in. What a mismatched tag team of overly animated freaks. Like the Tweedledee and Tweedledum of education. The Abbott and Costello of macaroni art. It is all very surreal. But thank Jesus, the Devil is gone, back to her job of introducing first-day preschoolers to their own personal abyss.

Ms. Pat and Ms. Patty have decked this room out pretty hard-core. It's like everything horrible about 1980s design has just exploded all over the walls. Posters of cartoon Caucasian families playing various sports. Party streamers crisscross from each corner of the room. A tiny library of ridiculous books about animals and the sounds they make. And a teeny tiny round table, circled by brightly colored plastic chairs with names taped to the back of each one: Michael P. Michael C. Jenny. David. Nicholas M. Nicholas A.

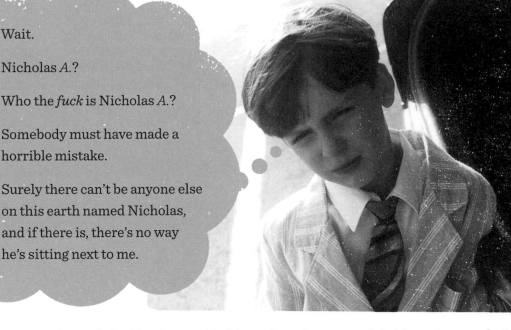

Wait.

Nicholas *A.*?

Who the *fuck* is Nicholas *A.*?

Somebody must have made a horrible mistake.

Surely there can't be anyone else on this earth named Nicholas, and if there is, there's no way he's sitting next to me.

Just then, a kid with a Snoopy T-shirt and maybe two teeth in his entire mouth sits down in the seat marked for Nicholas A. There's the son of a bitch who stole my first name. It's my first time realizing that I'm not special in this world and that I'm *certainly* not the only kid with the name Nicholas. By the stunned look on his face as he stretches his neck to read my name, he's having the same earth-shattering revelation. "Are you

Nicholas too?" he asks me shakily, as if he's making first contact with an alien. "Yes," I reply. He then proceeds to jump off the seat, pick it up with both hands, and carry it to the opposite side of the table, far away from me. I didn't like him anyway.

"Everyone find your name and take your seat!" the shorter Pat says with her hands on her childbearing hips. Her earrings are cats. I remember them clearly because the tails were straight up in the air, and there was a little indentation for a butthole. I kid you not. This woman wore them to teach preschool. She probably never even noticed it. A gag gift that she mistook for serious jewelry. Some of the kids are complete morons, it's obvious. A girl with pigtails sits right down in Michael P.'s seat, and Michael C. is telling her to move. Even though it's not even *his* seat. After a senselessly long period of tiny human panic, we finally are all on our butts.

"Do you know what this is?" Tall Pat asks the group as she holds up a bright red rotary telephone. She towers over us like a giraffe. She looks like a lady from one of those tribes that use brass rings to stretch their neck muscles over the course of thirty years. I imagine what an X-ray of her neck would look like. I had just learned about X-rays on *Sesame Street*, when Cookie Monster X-rayed Big Bird. Tall Pat was like a featherless Big Bird.

"This is a telephone that we can use to call your mommies and daddies!"

she tells us. Now, I'm only four years old, but I know she's lying because it's not plugged into anything. And my phone at home is plugged into the wall because that's where the phone calls come from. This bitch is lying to us in the first five minutes of our school career. And it causes me to cry. Out of nowhere, I lose it. The salty sadness is spilling from my eyes. Her dirty no-good deception has reduced me to tears. The next thing that happens is fucking unbelievable, but I swear to God it happened. I stand up and point at her. Almost as if I have no control of my finger. And directing my tiny preschool digit at her face, I utter something I've never said to anyone, let alone an adult. It's a word I heard on the playground.

"Fibber!" I cry.

"No, no. This is . . . this is a phone we can use!" she panics, picking up the prop phone with a faux smile. She fingers the rotary, pretending to dial my mom, and I know it. "Mrs. Megalis, this is Ms. Patty, Nicholas's teacher!" she says, to no one. Does this loon think I'm so unworldly as to not pick up on this charade? "Let me talk to her!" I demand in my most threatening voice, a high-pitched sort of yelp.

"Yes, yes, he's doing just fine! And he misses you too!" she says to my nonexistent mother. At this point, I am kind of almost humiliated for both of us.

"I want my mom!" I explode.

Snot pouring from my nose, I stomp my feet around in a circle like a wind-up toy soldier. I've had it with this fibber and her fibber school and all of these idiot kids. This has been the worst fifteen minutes of my entire life.

She bids adieu to my fake mother and hangs up the phone. "Okay, let's try to calm down. Do you want to learn about animals?" she pleads, leaning down beside me to instill some sort of trust. Her education partner, the shorter, dumpier woman of the same name, hands her *The Wonderful World of Animals*. I imagine at this point both of them are deeply regretting their decision to become teachers.

I somehow manage to calm down when she opens the book to a watercolor of a rhinoceros. I take the book from her hands and fall into a trance. Damn it, I love this rhino. He's so fat. And those horns are so sharp. Look at how he drinks from a pond, unmoved, as a little bird sits on top of his butt. Next thing I know, preschool is over. I'm drinking apple juice from a box and eating a cheese sandwich next to a kid who's licking peanut butter off of his knee. My Spider-Man book bag goes over my shoulders, slightly heavier than when I got here with the addition of a pencil eraser.

We all line up at the door to greet our parents. Nicholas A. is standing in front of me, facing the wrong way. He's glaring right at my face, point blank, because four-year-olds have no concept of space and no clue how to be normal, functional human beings yet. His mom calls his name, and we both look up. "I'm Nicholas too. We have the same name," I look up and tell her proudly. She nods politely and takes her son away. It's my turn now. My mom turns the corner and comes into the doorway to pick me up. She waves excitedly at me, and she's got tears in her eyes. I didn't know why she was crying at the time, but I know now that it's because she's my mom. And that's what moms do. They cry.

"How was your day, sweetheart?" she asks me. I don't miss a beat. I tell her the truth. "It was hell." Time stops moving. A bouncing ball drops from a boy's hand and rests midair. The hands of the classroom clock melt and drip down the wall like a

Dalí painting. I have opened up a wormhole in the space-time continuum with one four-letter word: "H-E-double hockey sticks," as the kids say. You see, this is a Catholic school. It's actually a church illegally zoned to be a school, if you wanna get technical. And in a Catholic school, unless you're reading a Bible passage, you just don't say that word. *Especially*, if you're a child. It's a no-no if there ever was one.

"What did you say?" Tall Pat, the class giraffe, says, her teeth clamped together with restrained rage. She leans in a little closer. Her nostrils are flared. Her perfume, nauseating. "I said it was hell." *Slap*. Right across my face. Not even a split second to brace for it. A wave of stinging pain rushes through my cheeks. There's no time to cry, no time to react, before my birth-giver steps in between the giraffe and me like a human barricade, my mother's tiny body, a wedge between the attacker and the victim. "Don't you *ever* touch my son!" my mother howls. Mom is barely up to this woman's breasts, but she delivers a verbal blow akin to an uppercut from Muhammad Ali in his prime. You ever seen those videos of Jane Goodall getting blitzed by the mother chimpanzee after messing with her babies? Imagine if the mother chimpanzee had sunglasses on the top of her head and car keys in her right hand. Now, my mother didn't lay a finger on this woman. But her finger got pretty close. "I will take you down," she cautions my intimidated teacher one last time, as she grabs my hand and chaperones me out of that school *forever*.

On the car ride home, we don't speak of it. Instead, I listen to popular children's performer Raffi sing about a beluga whale. Knowing my mother after all these years, I can almost guarantee that she was quietly proud that day, maybe even smiling from the front seat, out of view. My mom is a fighter. No, a protector. Five feet tall and ready to pounce.

Take that, Jane Goodall.

GODSPEED YOU DIRTY PUSSY

I've always been an animal lover. A fuzz hustler. A fur freak.

Animals of all shapes and varieties, I dig 'em. I'm especially fond of dogs. I have a shitty tattoo of a dog that I got in Cincinnati. It's an outline of a dog, actually. So there's no telling what the breed is. It's just a generic canine shape. That was the whole point. No breed, no discrimination. All dogs created equal. And if you squeeze the end of the tattoo, it aligns with a little brown mole that looks like the dog's butthole. It's a cute parlor trick. Something for the kids.

When I was born, my mom had a cat named Ozzy. Yes, named after the perpetually intoxicated rock 'n' roller. Apparently, he had just had a career resurgence. The guy, not the cat. I was too little to remember this, but my mom says the two Ozzys shared a lot in common. Ozzy the cat was blind in one eye, so he stumbled when he walked. And he slept all day, as if hungover from a night of rock 'n' roll shenanigans. The cat once climbed up my mom's leg in a rainstorm and scratched her boob so badly that she had to go to the emergency room. My dad wrapped her titty in a Kinks T-shirt and

sat with her in the waiting room of Allegheny Hospital. My parents swear it was then and there they realized they were not "cat people."

But the cats kept coming. Ozzy got hit by a kid on a tricycle and died in front of the mailbox with one paw raised to the sky as if to say, "You finally got me." He had burned through all nine of his lives before my second birthday. My dad dug a hole on the side of the house and buried Ozzy in that old Kinks T-shirt. Dad told me that it rained that day, and lightning struck a tree in the front yard right in the middle of his tearful eulogy. Both Ozzys would have been proud. How incredibly rock 'n' roll.

Enter: Erma. My dad found her in a blizzard outside of a Giant Eagle grocery store, seeking shelter under an abandoned shopping cart. She moved in with us and never quite fit the family. She was timid. My mom blasted her Carly Simon tape. My dad shouted in Greek at my grandmother in the kitchen. I was three years old, carrying the fuzzball around by her neck, her head about to pop off like a grape. At this point, a wintry death wasn't looking so bad. Erma was always up on the windowsill, her hands on the glass like a prisoner. She hated us. Absolutely couldn't stand us. It was show and tell at my preschool, and I dressed to the nines in a clip-on tie and light-up sneakers. I carried Erma across the parking lot to the playground, where my classmates were lined up from tallest to shortest, and she was already desperately wiggling around in my arms. I squeezed a little tighter. Michael Manhanton, the kid with the horrible breath, was about to present. He moved out of line, holding a potato with a smile drawn on it, and proudly showed it to his peers. Everyone clapped except for me. I couldn't clap while holding the hostage. I stepped up from the line and looked around at my classmates, who were all anxious to pet the cat. I opened my mouth to introduce Erma, and she was gone. She pushed her way out of my grasp and shot up and over my arms like a cork from a

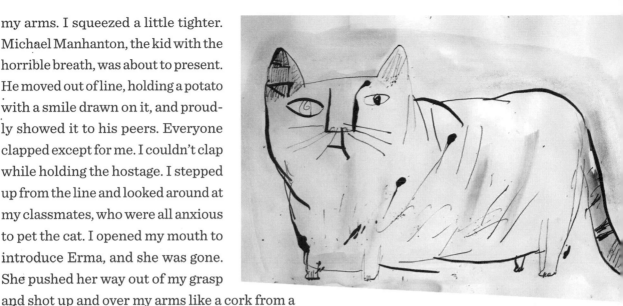

champagne bottle. She landed about five feet away and disappeared into the trees. The woods swallowed her that day. My dad drove around the neighborhood a few times and gave up. Wasn't meant to be. I cried all the tears I had in my body and then forgot about it over some chocolate chip pancakes. Thanks, Mom.

Ladies and gentlemen, I present to you—Nala. I named her after a character from *The Lion King*. She was another stray. My parents apparently didn't learn their lesson. She was in good shape when my dad brought her in. She was fat, actually. We put signs up all over the neighborhood—CAT FOUND—but nobody called. Then one day, I woke up and saw my old man out the window, just standing with his arms crossed in front of a rosebush in our front yard. I hurried downstairs and out the screen door. There, under the rosebush, all adorable and shit, was Nala and her ten newborn kittens. One of them was dead. My dad didn't want me to worry, so he said the cat was asleep. But I knew. "Don't tell Mommy yet," Dad pleaded. But it was too late. Mommy was standing behind us with an exhausted expression. "No wonder she was so fat," Mom said. Yep. My dad put an ad in the paper: "Nine kittens to good homes." One afternoon, a beautiful gay man with a Dalí mustache and his morbidly obese partner showed up in a Lincoln Town Car and adopted all of them. My dad says they named them after Hollywood sirens. Greta, Grace, Ava, Ingrid. They lived in an old schoolhouse and sent us photographs of the kittens every Christmas for years.

The fourth (and final) feline to claw its way into my life was Boo. I named him myself on Halloween night. My grandfather, an old-school Pennsylvania farmer, had a knocked-up tabby on his hands and was minutes from drowning the litter in the creek. My mom talked him out of it, and we adopted one of the boys. The rest ended up in a fancy pet shop outside of Pittsburgh, probably all sold at $400 a pop, with little pink and blue bows on their necks. When we picked up Boo on Halloween night, he was skinny. He looked like a furry skeleton. He was so tiny, my dad could hold him in his palm and close his fingers. He was almost too small to exist on this planet.

Mom wasn't ecstatic about Boo living at home with my baby sister, so he'd have to be a studio cat. Boo would chill in my dad's hellhole of an art space, 1520 Oak Street. Mountains of Xeroxes, empty paint cans, markers without caps, soiled T-shirts, shattered mirrors, antique telephones, speaker cables, Perry Como cassettes, and expired yogurt cups. Anywhere I stepped, I broke something further. "Art is war, Nicky. Art is war," my dad once preached while he squeezed blood out of a gash on his thumb onto a painting of Jesus. My dad was a hoarder. Still is. He'll bring home a box of dirt if he knows he can use it somehow.

Boo would sit perched on the gigantic piles of Dad's garbage like a vulture while I played guitar and my dad painstakingly animated television segments. Hunched over a miniature house, holding the remote to a 16-millimeter-film camera in one hand and a cup of coffee in the other, my dad worked into the night while Boo and I played like idiots. Boo was a fantastic listener. "Boo, I'm going to be a musician. I can play a ton of songs on my guitar. Do you want to hear the songs again, Boo?" I'd shout at him. The poor cat, desperate for a break from my incessant shrieking, would just sit there with tired eyes and his head in his stomach, half-asleep, while I strummed dissonant, tuneless shit on my oversized electric guitar.

As I got older, and better at guitar, Boo was still there on his garbage throne. My best audience. Never complaining, never walking out. I learned how to play music in that studio, in front of that cat. While my dad worked, I grew into the guitar that was once too big to hold. My fingers could wrap around the neck now. And I was making something that actually sounded like *music*. Those summer days, spent without air conditioning in the back room of my dad's chaos chamber with a dirty cat by my side are the stuff childhood is made of. Just a kid hanging out with a filthy cat.

After being banished to the studio, Boo sort of did his own thing for the next few years. Boo was hooking up with a sexy lady cat that lived in the alley behind the building. She lived under a drainpipe, and she smelled better than Boo, who lived indoors. My dad's friend Jay would come feed Boo when we couldn't be there. Jay was sneaking fresh fish and deli cuts to the cat. He even secretly took him to the vet and got him all checked out and paid for it himself. He was falling in love with Boo. His secret buddy. My dad took notice of Jay's over-affection and offered him full ownership of the cat. When I found out, it broke my heart. But it also made sense. Boo scratched the shit out of my sister, and my mom was developing allergies. Dad would come home from the studio with a little fur on his shirt, and my mom's nose would gush blood. Boo had to go. And Jay would give him a better home. They had a stronger bond.

ERMA

OZZY

On a very rainy day in the steel city, my dad and I pulled our Ford Explorer up to Jay's house and handed him the cat through my passenger window. I was too sad to say goodbye, so I said, "See ya." What a baby. Boo lived his entire life with Jay. Twenty goddamn years! Jay fed him only market-fresh seafood and invested tens of thousands of dollars into experimental medicine to treat Boo's diabetes. Last year, on another very rainy day in New York City, my dad called and told me Boo had moved on from this earth. I hadn't seen him since the day we dropped him off, but I couldn't help crying. I called Jay and thanked him for giving Boo the best life a cat could have.

Godspeed, you dirty pussy.

NALA

AN HONORARY JEW

"Excuse me, sir, are you Jewish?"

A friendly voice from my peripheral. I turn. A thin man in a long black coat and black hat reaches his hand out to shake mine. He's in his midtwenties or early sixties; it's hard to tell because of his enormous beard. His eyes are warm and sweet, his face is soft behind his facial bush. If I have a five o'clock shadow, then this guy's beard is clocking in at 11:45 p.m.

Across the street, a young kid is slammed onto the hood of a cop car. "Stop resisting! Stop resisting!" the officer screams as the kid spouts various four-letter words. A man selling grapefruit watches the scene from a folding chair. "Stop resisting!" A lone grapefruit falls from the top of the pile and rolls into the gutter. A bird shits on it. A rat falls in love.

"Are you Jewish?" he repeats, advancing his hand closer into my personal space. I accept, and we lock mitts. His hand is definitely moisturized. Smooth as silk and honey. Mine, on the other hand, is dry and rough and tobacco-stained. I am sort of embarrassed, to be quite honest. I should take better care of my freakin' hands.

"No, I'm not," I say politely. I don't want to disappoint him, but I can see his spirit disintegrate before my very eyes. His hand pulls away, and he smiles despite the major bummer bomb I have just dropped onto his whole day. "Have a good day." And just like that, he turns away. He's done with me. Now I feel crushed, like I've done something horribly wrong. Maybe I should have lied. I could have said I was, and he would never know the difference. But no, I don't speak any Hebrew. I don't know jack shit about being Jewish.

Beyond Woody Allen, I am Jew-clueless.

An old man in a black jacket walks by, and it happens again. "Excuse me, sir, are you Jewish?" The guy shakes his head no and keeps on walking and smoking a stupid-looking pipe. I always laugh when I see a pipe. It's just ridiculous. It's extravagant; it's unnecessary. It's an extra step to getting nicotine into your bloodstream. I don't have time for that shit. Give me a cigarette. Hell, give me a nicotine IV.

All day long, this guy stands on the corner of Nostrand and Eastern Parkway. He's probably out there at nine in the morning, but I wouldn't know because I haven't seen nine in the morning since I was in high school. I work for myself. No boss, no rules, at home in my living room. I direct commercials. Or at least that's what I tell people with money. I'm a goofball who happened to achieve some sort of "success" or whatever on the Internet. Everybody's making it big on the World Wide Web these days. It's a hotbed for losers and nutjobs who have extraordinarily random and bizarre talents. It's a nightmare, this digital age. But thank God for it, or else you wouldn't be reading this book.

I look Jewish. I think I do, at least. Now don't get your balls in an uproar, because the fact is, I love the Jewish people more than I can put into words. They are the source of some of the most inspired and brilliant

comedy, music, literature, and food in the history of humans. Now, as my Greek aunt Georgia explained to me during one of her many manic episodes of hyperanalysis and bat-shit craziness, Jews and Greeks are a lot alike. The great pulse of anxiety flows through our veins, and our hearts beat in the same sort of rhythm. We are great thinkers, fueled by self-reflection and obsessiveness, powered by agitation and drama. We work hard to make life better for our families and friends, and when we love you, we love you to death. And also, a matzo ball is something I would strangle someone over. I just love the stuff.

New York City is a spectacularly Jewish town. It's a Jew hub. And it's always been comforting to me. Maybe it was ingrained in me when I was a young kid. After my preschool incident, my mom had me enrolled in *another* Catholic school. Still thought it would be a good idea. An "alternative" approach to education, if you will. On a particularly bitter winter morning, Sister Mary Eunice called me into her office after prayer time to "discuss a critical issue." She didn't have the heat running in her office. In fact, the whole building was frozen over. From the hallways to the chapel. It's as if they kept it cold to keep the students docile and gelid. Your body slows down in those temperatures. (Fun fact: You can put a bumblebee in your refrigerator for a half hour and when you take it out, it will be calm enough to tie a string around. Then you have a little leash for your bee.)

Sister Mary Eunice was as cold as her office. She had blue hands, and her lips were thin and cracked. One of her eyes stared me down, and the other drifted like a dead goldfish in a murky tank. That eye was messed up. "Nicholas, now I understand you are Jewish?" Apparently, one of my teachers started a rumor that I was a Jewish kid going to a Catholic school because it was cheaper than the other private schools in town. I didn't know about this. My mother told me all about it when she pulled me out. "They thought you were Jewish. They said you looked Jewish," my mom said as she sped out of the parking lot on my last day. I was enrolled for maybe two weeks. Judgmental pricks. "Jewish, Greek, white, black, alien, Hobbit. What does it matter?" Mom asked rhetorically. She was right. None of it matters. We are all the goddamn same. Sister Mary Eunice died in a helicopter explosion a few years ago. She was sightseeing in the Sahara when the pilot lost control and slammed into a herd of mating camels. I wonder if when she got to Heaven God pulled her into his office to "discuss a critical issue."

Now here I am in my underwear, smoking a cigar on my fire escape, staring out into beautiful Brooklyn. I've been here for a half-decade, and I love it like a wife. My favorite bagel shop in the world is on the far right corner. I can smell the bagels from my bed. Directly across from the bagel place is a little Jewish deli. A guy named Ariel, with huge muscles and, from what he tells me, a huge penis, is the resident butcher. He cuts the corned beef superthin for me, and he knows more about me than I know about myself. His little wife is a mind reader. She knows when I've lost money. Or when I've just had sex. She's got this deep gaze that cuts through your eyeballs and into your heart. "Are you Jewish?" Ariel asks. He asks me every day. Literally every single day. He knows I'm not Jewish, but he asks me anyway. I don't know why. "No, Ariel," I laugh. "I'm a Greek Orthodox guy." He hands me a plastic baggie filled with stinky corned beef, and he puts a Sharpie through the bar code to cancel out the sale.

"It's free today, my friend. Free for the Greek Jew."

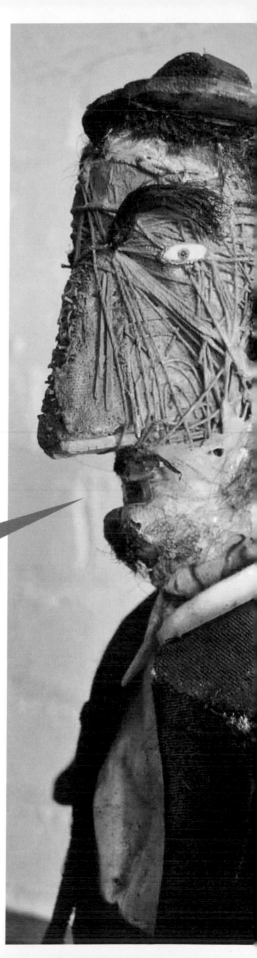

Beautiful. I want that on my tombstone: THE GREEK JEW.

Now don't get me wrong, I love being Greek. It's half of my blood. The messed up half. My dad's side. With the mental illness and whatnot. The other half, on my ma's side, is a hodgepodge of German, Irish, and Polish, and probably some other weird shit. I'm proud to be a hybrid. I am a creation of my parents, whom I love oh so dearly. I am my dad's nose and my mom's teeth. I am my dad's insomnia and egomania, and my mother's powerful flatulence. A product of two insane people who collided.

Today I'm shooting a video for the internet in my living room.

My very Catholic grandmother calls in the middle of the shoot. I'm dressed head-to-toe like a prostitute. Sorry, that's crude. A working girl. I'm dressed like I work the streets. My eyelids are heavy with blue makeup and false lashes. My lips are succulent and cherry-colored. Wow, I'm turning myself on. I am wearing my girlfriend's dress. I look beautiful. "Grandma, I love you too. But I'm shooting a video. I'm going to have to call you back later." If only she could see my platinum-blonde wig and padded bra. I look like her worst nightmare. She would douse me in holy water and call out for the devil to release my soul.

"Make sure to say a prayer for Uncle Lawrence. His bowels are acting up."

I kid you not, my grandmother is talking about Uncle Larry's bowels. It's not like he has colon cancer. Knock on wood. His bowels are simply acting up. "Okay, Grandma. No problem. I love you so much. Bye!" Readjust my wig, fix my eyelashes a bit, push up my bra. Damn, I look good. The video I am shooting today is for the world to see. To discuss in a public forum, praised, slammed, and dissected by total strangers. A song that I wrote and produced booms out of my computer speakers. It's a rap song about being "fabulous."

i am so fabulous 𝄆
you are so drab-ulous 𝄆
if style is a weapon 𝄆
Yo. you gonna get stabbed—ulous

Some deep shit, ain't it? I'm proud of myself. Those are some incredibly profound lyrics. I take a sip of my ice water with a hint of lemon. I have stopped drinking alcohol completely. I haven't been this sober since I was a newborn baby. It's strange, and often boring. But it's the clearest my head has been in a while, and it feels pretty good to remember conversations and large purchases the next day. I can't tell you how many times I've woken up on the floor of my living room, fully dressed, with a new microwave oven under my arm. Or a French press. Or a flat-screen television. It's a thing I do when I'm royally plastered. I buy stuff. It's a nasty habit to have when you really don't have a lot of money. If money is the root of the tree of all evil, alcohol is the watering can.

I'm rapping into the fish-eye lens like a Beastie Boy in drag. My lips look juicy in the monitor. What a fucking weirdo. Just when I'm getting into a groove, just when the shoot is getting good . . . the clogs. The damn clogs. Like a horse with wooden shoes on all four feet. Like a one-man stampede. My upstairs neighbor is off the couch, and this means the shoot is over. Edith is a fifty-something French lesbian who used to be a dancer. Once in the stairwell, she shook my hand and told me in her thick accent that my hair was "breathtaking." Her girlfriend is a painter.

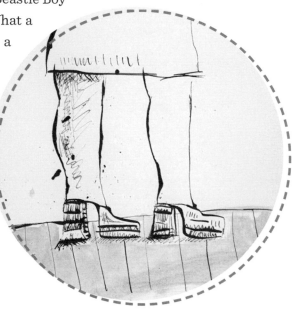

They both are around four feet tall, unemployed, and spend their entire day within the confines of their one-bedroom apartment. Edith wears wooden clogs everywhere she goes. Her floor is my ceiling, so I hear it all day long. When they are away in France for two months each year, I often sit and close my eyes and just soak in the silence. Because the rest of the year, it sounds like a fucking bowling alley right above my head. Sometimes she is running. Full speed. Faster than you should or even could run in an apartment of that size. How does one even accumulate speed? It's four hundred fucking square feet of space.

I looked at her thick little legs up close once when we were both getting our mail. She's packing power in those shanks. She's a mini-Godzilla in blocky shoes, clomping around. Edith and her girlfriend cackle wildly like hyenas all through the night. They drink and break wine glasses and scream out charades guesses. And when they have an argument, it's never just a friendly disagreement. It's either ecstatic laughter or explosive yelling. Sometimes at four in the morning, I will be in a deep sleep, and in my dream I am on a yacht in the middle of a chocolate pudding ocean, being blown

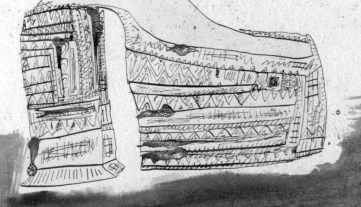

by a girl who looks like a unicorn. Like, she actually has a horn growing out of her forehead. Maybe it's just a disease or a tumor or some shit. I don't know for sure. I don't write my dreams. When all of a sudden, I am jolted awake by something that sounds like a bookshelf being thrown across the fucking room above me. Edith. She runs from above my bedroom to above my kitchen. Then back from above my kitchen to above my bedroom. She is sobbing hysterically. The floorboards are thin; I can hear every word. "You don't fucking love me anymore, well then fuck you! I don't need you, you bitch!" she screams. Her girlfriend barks something back in French, and I squeeze the pillow over my eardrums. Glasses breaking. Some more clogging around the place. Then something large falls. Then another glass breaks. Then clogging. She has the clogs on every *goddamn* second of every *goddamn* day. I fall back asleep. But of course, the unicorn girl has retreated to her castle made of popcorn. I will never finish my blowjob. C'est la vie.

One afternoon, I see Edith in the grocery store and she's got the clogs on. Of course.

They're superglued to her feet. I'm not really in the mood to chat, so I pretend to be superinterested in a particular brand of spaghetti sauce. "Hello, Nathan!" she says excitedly. She still doesn't know my name, even though I've introduced myself maybe eleven times just this year alone. I don't correct her. I just smile and wave. She's coming my way. She's clogging over now. I try not to look down at her shoes, at the very culprits of my sleeplessness. The funny thing is, even if I were to ever say something about how loud her shoes were, she wouldn't understand. She's so oblivious. So incredibly out of touch. "Nathan, I'm having some friends over for a party. Do you and your girlfriend wish to come?" I wish to remove your clogs, that's what I fucking wish. "When is it, Edith? That sounds delightful." Did I just say *delightful*? I just used *delightful* in an actual sentence. I'm disgusted with myself. "It's this Saturday night. Bring your girlfriend, Catherine." She remembers my girl's name but not mine. Maybe she likes her. Maybe she has a crush on her. Oh, God. "Okay, I think we can swing it. See you then!" I pick up a jar of pasta sauce and put it into my basket. I don't even like this sauce. I just need to get the hell out of here.

"Okay, so Edith cornered me in the grocery store," I tell Catherine as she sits down on our couch. I still have glitter in my hair from an alien video I shot today,

and she picks it out of my hair like a monkey. "And?" she asks. "And we're going to a party on Saturday in her apartment." Catherine is exhausted from a full day of actual work. She does the nine-to-five dance in a big office with a boss. I could never do what she does. I'm such a slacker, it's unbelievable. Her head falls back, and she just sighs. "Okay, I guess that's cool." She is defeated. She knows there's no way out of it because we are too nice to cancel. "Maybe one of us can break their leg or get really sick with the flu," I say. "Maybe I can throw myself in front of a bus and we won't have to go. I don't want to die, necessarily. I just want to be too injured to leave the apartment." "Nick, shut up. We're going."

Saturday night has arrived, and I am dreading this party. I don't know why I agreed to go. I'm standing in the mirror dressed in the only button-down shirt I own that isn't stained or missing a button. Catherine is wearing the dress that I wore in my video, except she is wearing it much, much better. I can already hear the commotion upstairs. Feet are moving around in circles, definitely dancing of some sort. Laughter and the clinking of glasses. The music is strange and actually beautiful. Upright bass, for sure. But it doesn't sound like it's coming out of a stereo. It sounds closer than that. More personal. "Let's go. It's now or never," I say. A deep breath. Exhale. Catherine looks beautiful. She takes my hand, and we make our grand journey up the one flight of stairs to Edith's apartment. Outside the door, the laughter is getting louder. In a mess of conversation and music, I can make out a few words here and there. "Oh, it's fantastic!" someone shouts. A man chimes in, "It's to die for!"

I knock, but no one answers. No one can hear us. Catherine presses the doorbell, but no answer. How could they hear us? I push the door just a little, and it opens wide. The lights are low and orange. Maybe twenty or thirty nicely dressed bodies are crammed into a living room, and a man plucks an upright bass in the corner. He smokes a pipe. A stupid, goofy pipe. A guy next to him in a purple jacket is playing an oboe or some shit. Everyone looks like characters that F. Scott Fitzgerald made up. A lady with huge teeth laughs into her cocktail. A man in a fedora is writing his phone number on a receipt for some guy he just met. "Call me sometime. We should have some fun." He rubs the man's hand gently. Everyone is older than us. Much older. While I'm just freshly twenty-five years old, the average age of this party is *forty*-five. It's controlled debauchery. Mature mischief. It's the kind of party that your parents would throw if they were just a tad bit spunkier. The star of the show is standing on her coffee table, telling a funny story in her dense, French tongue. "So I took her to the zoo and she said, 'Edith, *you* should be in the monkey cage because you're the one who's the monkey!'" I'm not quite sure if that was even a proper punch line, but her friends all laugh hysterically.

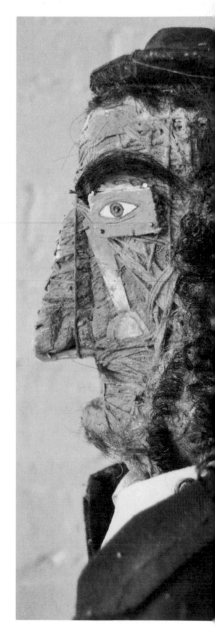

"Nathan! Catherine!" She spots us and jumps from the table. She stomps over in her fat clogs and gives us both fancy Euro kisses on each cheek. She smells good. Her lips are soft on my cheek. Her eyes are sweet and kind. I feel bad that I ever felt any animosity toward her. She's just some lady who happens to wear very loud shoes. Her girlfriend runs from the kitchen with a tray full of cookies, and everyone cheers. "I'm so glad you two could make it. I want you to meet my friend Ariel," Edith says.

The name clicks in my brain. I know an Ariel too. There's no way that this could be the same Ariel, though. My Ariel is a Jewish butcher whose penis is apparently the size of a small ocean liner.

She produces her Ariel, or rather pulls a man out of another conversation with one quick yank on his velvet jacket sleeve. Ariel. Holy shit. *The* Ariel. From the deli counter. He smiles, showing his crooked teeth, and he gives me a hug and a kiss. "Ariel! So good to see you. This is my girlfriend, Catherine." Ariel kisses Catherine. Not on her cheek. On the lips. If this guy didn't slice my meat every day, I probably would be upset. But he's the greatest dude in the world. And I fucking love him. "What a beautiful Jewish couple!" he says with a wink.

Edith looks at me, and then at Catherine, and then back at me, and she throws her hands up in the air, almost knocking a man flat on his ass. "You're *Jewish*!" she says excitedly. "I'm Jewish too! And so is Esther! Oh, this is wonderful. This is so wonderful!" She grabs Catherine's arm with one hand and mine with the other, and she pulls us into the thick of the party. I don't drink anymore, but I'm getting drunk just being around these people. Just the air in the room is enough to intoxicate me. These people. These older people. They are beautiful; they are happy. They are making me feel like *I'm* the old man. "Everyone dance with my new Jewish friends!" Edith howls. The party erupts in jubilant insanity. Catherine gives me the look. The look that people have been giving me all my life. The look that says, "You're nuts." And I love it. I give her a look back. The look that says, "Nobody needs to know. Just smile and pretend you're Jewish with me."

The upright bassist smokes his pipe. The guy on the oboe or whatever is going wild. A lady in a floral print scarf is bragging loudly over the music that she slept with Bobby Kennedy. I am eating challah bread and stomping my feet around. I'm an honorary Jew. My dream come true. The night is young. Edith and Ariel are slow dancing. Esther is drinking wine from the bottle on the lap of a man who looks old enough to have taught algebra to my grandfather. "Try these on. I give you a pair. They are from France. I give you this pair. They are for a man; they don't fit me." Edith hands me a pair of wooden shoes. Clogs. They fit beautifully. I slide into them like a hot knife in butter. They feel natural. They feel incredible. Like I was born to wear them. Catherine shakes her head as I dance. She blows me a kiss, and I scoop it out of the air and swallow it.

Tonight, there is no one downstairs with a pillow over his head, wishing that it would just stop.

I am the one who clogs now.

MY CIGARETTE SUMMER

Aunt Georgia wasn't just *seated* on my Yia Yia's couch.

She was *merged* with the couch. Her ample body seeped into every crevice, making her one with the sofa. It was where she completed Bible-sized crossword puzzle magazines and smoked incessantly.

I never saw her without a lit cigarette. She chain-smoked these long, skinny fags that came in a fancy pink pack. Luxury cancer. For some reason, only aunts smoke those kinda cigarettes. Are they marketed toward aunts? Do aunts have some sort of secret word-of-mouth club where they all gather around and suck on fancy cigarettes and sigh heavily at each other? Would we decipher the location of their hideout if we read between the lines of their crossword puzzles?

Georgia was watching *The Price Is Right* on a television set that was probably manufactured before Bob Barker celebrated his first birthday. My sweaty Greek dad

stood beside the TV, smacking it with his palm to fix the picture and muttering something along the lines of, "It's 1996 . . . no air conditioning? Come on, Mom. . . ." Yia Yia's house was piping hot during Ohio summers, and the plastic coating on all the furniture made it worse. You would sit down in your own stinky butt sweat and just sort of boil in it. If you fell asleep on your face, someone would have to pry you off the plastic like an overcooked Greek flapjack.

I was always turned on by cigarettes. Obsessed, even. The smell of them, the way they looked hanging off of my aunt's fat lips. Even the lipstick marks on all the butts in the Snow White ashtray. (Literally, a promotional ashtray for the children's film that my Yia Yia picked up at a garage sale sometime before my dad popped out of the womb.) I wanted to get my hands on a pack and suck them all down to the filter. I wanted to fill my tiny, precious seven-year-old lungs with the noxious smoke of twenty beautifully wrapped disease-sticks.

Now keep in mind, my Aunt Georgia was so out of touch, she was in another galaxy. She also had no kids of her own, so she spoiled the *hell* out of me. I once tricked her into buying me a *Penthouse* magazine by placing it facedown on the countertop at the neighborhood drugstore. She didn't even look at what it was. "Whatever Nicky wants!" she would cry out to my dad when he would try to talk sense into her. "He's the best there is!" she'd say. Aww. Aunt Georgia loved me. She still does. She's not dead.

Aunt Georgia would fall into a deep coma-like sleep and snore so loudly that I would have to watch TV with the captions on. God forbid a kid reads something once in a while though, right? While my aunt was unconscious and my dad cut Yia Yia's lawn with a rusty push-mower out front, I could very carefully, very slowly, pull Georgia's purse out from under the rolls on her left arm and steal a few smokes from her pack.

Walking on the sides of the staircase, where it was most quiet, I eased my way to the upstairs bathroom like the Pink Panther. The bathroom was bare. A miniature tattered painting of Saint Elias hung loosely from a bent nail in the mildewed tile wall above the bathtub. The bathroom stank like artificial cherry and black mold. Little slivers of used toilet paper that didn't quite make it into the toilet were always scattered around the bowl. Poor Yia Yia just didn't notice.

It was in this bathroom where I would take my first deep hit of a cigarette. The first kiss to begin a lifelong love affair. I propped the tiny window frame open with a shit-crusted plunger handle. Thick summer air and carbon monoxide permeated the commode. This was my clubhouse. A clubhouse where you took a dump. I usually only had one match on me, so I would light three cigarettes off of each other and vacuum them down to my knuckles like a seven-year-old crackhead.

It's been a hot minute since I've enjoyed a cig like I did in 1996. At twenty-five, a cigarette is like a cup of coffee. I don't really want one, but I need one. It's something to do while I'm on an awful phone call, something to occupy my hands when I'm not sending a text message. It's a little friend who won't go away but you can't stand to be without. The flames of my romance may have died down, but the memories are burned into me.

Nineteen ninety-six was my cigarette summer.

TWENTY-THREE YEARS OLD, FULL OF BAD DECISIONS, AND BROKE AS A JOKE

On the night of my twenty-fourth birthday, my life changed forever.

Yeah, I guess you could say that your life changes every day. You change your mind, you change your pants, you change your oil. Whatever. But twenty-four was an atomic bomb of a change.

It was the day I busted my neck.

One of my best friends from Cleveland had just made the move to New York City. Timmy. He was fresh off a fifteen-hour bus ride with a wide smile on his face and this insane notion that he would conquer an unconquerable beast. When you first move to New York, everything is flipping fantastic! Jazz music on every street corner. The homeless dancing around on their crutches like it's a goddamn musical.

The sun is bright and hot on your face. You're eating a pretzel and skipping around like Gene Kelly because you haven't been crushed yet. Give it five years. Hell, give it a month.

I wanted to show Timmy around New York. My New York. See, everybody has their own version. Forget the Statue of Liberty and Katz's Deli. Screw the Top of the Rock. I took Timmy to eat at the two-buck hot dog shop that gets shut down every three months for health-code violations. We people-watched on Delancey under the Williamsburg Bridge, drunk off our asses at two in the morning on a Monday. Dined and ditched at a taco place after googling it midmeal only to discover that they were famous for serving feral cat. This was my New York. Twenty-three years old, full of bad decisions, and broke as a joke. Literally, $14.37 in my bank account, pouring ketchup on ramen noodles and calling it spaghetti.

Timmy is a skateboarder. A damn good one. He's skinny with spider legs and can pop an ollie higher than any kid I know. His skateboard stance is so strange and beautiful. It makes him look like one of those tree-dweller monkeys you see on Animal Planet. He once jumped off a roof and broke his ass. That was the first time I had ever heard of someone breaking their ass. Timmy and I once spent an entire summer in a Burger King parking lot, skateboarding, whistling at old women, and fishing half-eaten cheeseburgers out of the garbage. Kids are idiots. Each and every last one of them. It's as if at birth we are programmed to be idiots, and then we spend the rest of our lives deprogramming.

It was the night of my twenty-fourth birthday, and I was spending it with Timmy and my long-suffering girlfriend. Good Lord, somebody give her a medal. The poor girl. We were seated in the back corner of a hole-in-the-wall Vietnamese restaurant on Baxter Street in Chinatown. It's always a sauna in there. The windows are perpetually foggy from fat Asian people sucking down boiling-hot noodles. And everyone's always coughing loudly. It's a flu incubator. If you're ever in the mood to get sick, pop a squat at Baxter Pho and breathe in deep, baby. Timmy ordered a beer, and I ordered five. It's my birthday. Might as well have some fun at my body's expense. We finished our soups and decided to skip the overpriced frat-boy-infested bars and headed right back to the comfort of my shoebox apartment, where Timmy was temporarily living while he hunted the internet for apartments that didn't do credit checks.

After the cake was cut, my saintlike girlfriend had to sit tableside in absolute horror while Timmy and I pounded back beers like we were contestants on a self-abuse game show. A case and a half of pisswater later, and we were walking into walls and speaking in tongues. I can vaguely remember trying to tell my sweet girlfriend, "I love you, thanks for the birthday cake," but it came out in some sort of half burp–half English hybrid-speak sounding something like "I laub, yooshe tan forteh borthdud cay." I was in no condition to be conscious, let alone step foot on a skateboard. But that's precisely what I was about to do.

I remember shouting something about stale potato chips at my girlfriend while she begged me to "just sit the fuck down." I definitely recall shattering a plate that had belonged to my great-aunt Melinda, who apparently stole it from Buckingham Palace on a walking tour. There was lots of explosive laughing, explosive puking, and heavy sighs from my sweet, miserable girlfriend.

I hate having to say "the next thing I know," but it's exactly the case. Literally, the next thing I know, I'm pushing off on my skateboard into the bitter wind. My eyes can't adjust to the darkness, and it probably doesn't help that I am intoxicated to the level of near-blindness. Timmy is still trying to get on his skateboard, drunk as a tequila worm, and skinny like one too. I'm laughing and coughing up birthday cake simultaneously, and my hair is whipping around my face. I think some neighborhood kids are drinking 40s on the stoop across the street because I hear one of them scream, "Look out, white boy!"

I taste gravel. I taste blood. Did I just die? Oh, God, I hope I'm not dead because I didn't file my taxes yet. Wait, here's my arm. I can move my arm to feel around and lift myself off the ground. I must have wiped out pretty hard.

My chin has a loose flap of dirty skin hanging off of it. My bottom front teeth are loose. I can push them around with my tongue. My head feels like a fishbowl, all sloshy. Slow footsteps behind me. A familiar, goofy monkey voice in my ear: "Duuuuuuuuuuude."

Today, my skateboard is home to a family of spiders as it sits dormant in the front closet of our apartment. I have since retired from the sport. Nearly one year later, I don't even cross the street without a chaperone. I've diagnosed myself with PTSD, or Post Traumatic Skateboarding Disorder. I have switched from booze to ginger ale, and my girlfriend has the pleasure of rubbing me down with that stinky-old-man menthol cream every night before bed.

Here's to twenty-five.
Cheers.

This OLD WOMAN is SMOKING a cigarette... in a FIREWORKS STORE?

The smell of sulfur fills the air.

Fat mushrooms of thick white smoke rise from their respective cardboard tubes. Little scraps of brightly colored tissue paper dance all around and fall to the lawn like snowflakes. It's August in North Carolina. And I'm addicted to fireworks.

"Get the hell away from that!" my mother yells. She's running toward me, full speed, galloping like a mama horse. "What the hell are you doing?!" she shouts, as she swats a lit Roman candle out of my hand. She grabs my arm, and we run for our lives as the abandoned Roman candle showers our backs with fire. I can feel the heat on my neck, singeing my little blond hairs. My mother lets out an animal shriek: "Shit! Shit! Shit!"

"Nick, enough is enough. Let's go!" my dad says, out of breath, as he jogs past us to extinguish the rogue explosive device. He's drained. He's had it. I can see it in his dark brown eyes. His soul is sucked. But how can he blame *me*? *He's* the one who got me into fireworks in the first place. The old man likes blowing shit up. What man *doesn't*? And I absolutely, without a doubt, inherited my pyromaniac genes from him. That Greek firebug bastard.

The old man brings me to a roadside fireworks shop and gives me a spending limit. He kneels down in the gravel parking lot and says, "You have fifty dollars. You can buy whatever you want. But Mom and I have to light them. If you so much as touch a pack of matches, you will not only be grounded, and all of the fireworks will be taken away, but you will also blow your hands off. And you will have only pieces of your hands left." It's pretty goddamn graphic, so I get the message loud and clear. I am given carte blanche. Complete free rein in the fireworks shop. But I'm not allowed anywhere near an open flame. Because my hands will be blown clean off the bone.

The tattered sign out front says it all: FIREWORKS: 50% OFF SALE. The font is made to look like a lit fuse. And the word *sale* is all in red and yellow, like a big explosion. I am transfixed. We make our way through the busted screen door, and my dad immediately steps on a cat. It lets out this horrific scream that feels like it could ignite all of the fireworks in the building.

"Oh, Jesus, I'm sorry!" my dad says, reaching down to pet the injured cat. The cat hisses at him and runs under the countertop to seek refuge from his torturer. A skinny old woman with pointy elbows and limp, bluish skin sits under a spasming fluorescent bulb affixed to a dangerously wobbly ceiling fan. The fan looks old enough to be the first prototype for ceiling fans. And it scares the shit out of me. I glance at the old woman's pencil neck and imagine the fan coming loose, falling, and then hacking off her head like a grape. Fountains of blood shooting all over us and the cat at her feet. Her dead hand still holding a Virginia Slim.

WAIT.

A cigarette? This old woman is smoking a *cigarette . . . in a fireworks store*? Gray embers fall off the cherry tip of the cigarette into an ashtray shaped like the state of North Carolina, next to a tupperware container filled to the brim with M-80s, on sale 50 percent off. While we're at it, why not douse the place with gasoline? Maybe light some candles and strike some flint? Maybe get a little campfire going? I'm only eight years old, but I know this is dangerous. She is very literally playing with fire.

My dad doesn't seem to notice. He's too busy digging through a box of bottle rockets. "These make the whistling noise, right?" he says, turning to face the woman. She's taking a deep draw off the Virginia Slim, breathing it in and taking her time to answer him, because in North Carolina, time is on your side. There's time for everything. It stands still. It crawls by like a heat-stroked May beetle on your front porch while you drink beer and think about the storm. You can't even feel it moving, if time moves at all. The shutters shake on the house. You sip your Budweiser from a bottle. Lightning draws lines in the horizon, and the wind pets your face, and time stands *still*.

"These whistle, right?" dad asks. Again.

"Now, look," she says slowly, as she gets up from her stool. It's as if she's been on that stool for thirty years and her body fused to it like creeping vines on a toolshed. It takes her a good minute and a half to hoist her bag of bones from the stool and make her way around the countertop. The cat makes his move and jumps up onto the empty stool to take her place, as if he's guarding it from another elderly woman who might want to sell fireworks.

She puts her cigarette out on the ground and crushes it with her tiny sandals. The way she walks is strangely inhuman, as if she's a grasshopper in loose-fitting human skin, still getting adjusted to controlling her host body. She is bowlegged and uncomfortably scrawny. Her epidermis is carved out with thick wrinkles. She looks vaguely like a topographical map. Fatty deposits on her neck appear to be little hills. Her lips are like a crater, painted bright red around the rim. Her breasts are empty ocean basins, dry and flat for millions of years.

The old woman's hair, or what's left of it, is dyed red. Bright red, like Lucille Ball. Large sections of her scalp poke through the patches of thin, spiked hair. It is reminiscent of a Barbie's hair after a dog has gotten to it and ripped most of it out. Upon closer inspection, I notice that on her battered T-shirt is a lifelike drawing of a polar bear, and upon even closer inspection, the polar bear's left eye is missing, and one of her nipples is poking through where the eye should be. It is so unbelievable that I cannot physically look away. My dad, oblivious to the nipple, strikes up a conversation like he always does, because my dad studies everyone he meets so that he can later use them in his own perfect, albeit psychotic, impersonations. "Polar bears, huh? You like them? You see, I've never met a polar bear, but I've always wanted to ride one! Would you ride a polar bear, or do they scare you?" He laughs and looks at her intensely. I look up at my old man, and he's drinking her in like a glass of North Carolina swamp water. I can see it in his face. He is absorbing this woman, committing her to memory. He is getting a new character to add to his book of weirdos, right here in this crappy little store on the side of the road.

The old woman doesn't entirely understand what's going on, go figure. But it's not because she's necessarily slow. It's because my dad isn't even really *saying anything*. You see, he's demonstrating a tactic that I've seen him use for as long as I can remember. The art of confusion. "You bombard someone with a bunch of information, whether it's questions or statements or whatever," he'd tell me. "And then you get anything you want. Because they're just overwhelmed by your *assault* on their brain! That's how I get free parking for baseball games, Nick. You just go up to the parking garage guy and tell him your shoes are in the stadium bathroom, and oh, yeah, they changed the wallpaper in the bathroom *six* times since the field opened in the '70s, and your buddy is in there with your ticket, and your wife is about to give birth to a baby girl, and then you compliment the parking garage attendant's shirt, and he's happy, and then you just drive your car in there and he tells you his life story and how he used to work at a zoo but they have better benefits at the parking garage, and by the end of the conversation, you've just parked your car for free."

My dad is a friggin' trip.

"I never rode a polar bear," she says grimly. I can only imagine what my dad will say on the car ride home. "She was impenetrable. She wasn't giving me anything to work with. But I'll do that character in my show. You watch. I'm writing her into the pilot." My dad, always pitching a show. Always making something. Always churning out ideas, no matter where or what from. He has this biological cocktail of perseverance, sleepless hustle, creative lunacy, and complete, uninhibited immaturity. He's the oldest baby I know.

"So, are these bottle rockets the ones that whistle?" my dad asks, reverting back to his original question and giving up completely on the polar bears. She points to the tiny hand-written sign that's taped to the front of the box. It says WHISTLIG ROCKETS. She doesn't even say a word, she just points a bony finger at the sign. "Ah, okay. Got it," Dad says. He glances at me, and I know he sees the obvious misspelling. "Thank you for your help. We really appreciate it."

She just walks away without a word, reaches into her back pocket, and pulls out a new smoke to shove into her wrinkly mouth-hole. She hates us. Absolutely hates us and probably wants us to leave the store without buying anything. It's *that* strong a hate. She doesn't even want the sale, for God's sake. She just wants us to get the hell out of there. I wonder if it had anything to do with my dad's polar bear bullshit. Or maybe she's just a miserable old lady who works all alone in a fireworks shop on the side of the road.

My dad hands me a red plastic basket. It's like he's giving me the keys to Pyrovania, an incredible imaginary land where I can light shit on fire and watch it blow up. I love the way the fireworks smell. I hold them up to my nose and inhale, the sulfuric overload speeding through my nasal passages. I'm like an eight-year-old Tony Montana, except instead of cocaine it's plasterboard tubing filled with combustible powder.

What a little psycho.

WHEN YOU AREN'T MAKING SOMEBODY MONEY, THEY DON'T GIVE TWO FLYING MONKEY DICKS ABOUT YOU ←

My eyes are crusted shut, so I reach for a T-shirt and wipe them open.

"Where the hell are we?" I ask the blurry figures around me. I know it's my band from their body odor. "Phoenix. We're in Phoenix today, dude," Rich says. "Sorry, it's just hard . . . hard to keep track because everything looks the same out here." And it's true. It all looks the fucking same. If you would have told me we were in Texas, I would have believed you. If it weren't so goddamn hot, you could have lied and said Utah. The highways all blend together when you're driving for this long. The little towns have a bar and a gas station, a diner and a hair salon. The big towns have a Best Buy and a Subway restaurant and a McDonald's.

Ronnie's cellphone rings. Journey's "Don't Stop Believin'" plays through the tiny phone speakers. What a cornball. "Ronnie here," he says. "Uh-huh . . . okay . . . well, how's . . . do they know we are coming? Oh, they don't? They have no clue? This show was booked, what, three months ago, and they have no fucking clue that we're coming?" Oh, God. I know this call; I've heard it maybe six times since we left Ohio.

It's the call Ronnie receives from the local promoter to let us know that the club has absolutely no idea that my band is coming to play. The club will be on its regular schedule, with no one working the sound board and no posters hung up anywhere to alert people that my band is in town. It's a result of poor communication between my managers and the idiots who run the club circuit. When you aren't making somebody money, they don't give two flying monkey dicks about you.

We pull into a Burger King parking lot to get a few of those rubbery gray discs they pass off as hamburgers, and that's where I completely lose my shit. I climb out of the van and slam the door on my friends. "Fuck it!!!!!" I scream at the top of my lungs. A morbidly obese man in a wheelchair stares at me from his window seat inside the restaurant, because apparently my voice has pierced the glass. There, that feels better. I mouth "sorry" at the man and give him a friendly little smile. Everything is okay. Everything is okay. This tour is going to get better. Once we get to Los Angeles, we're going to get a record deal. And everything will be okay.

"Dude, what's wrong?" Timmy asks, stepping out of the van with an unlit cigarette hanging from his lips. He puts his arm around me. A gesture of compassion. A good friend. Another little reminder of why I'm on tour to begin with. To spend it with people like Timmy. "Nothing, man. All good. This . . . this fucking show isn't going to happen," I tell him, reaching for a cigarette of my own. The famous traveling nicotine brothers. A cigarette for every occasion. A freakout, a celebration, premeal, postmeal. We love to smoke together. It's a bonding agent. "I know, man. It's bogus. This whole thing is bogus. But it's the best time we've ever had." And being a generally bored and boring Ohioan, I have to agree. It's the best time we've all *ever* had.

"Let's get tattoos," I suggest. Out of nowhere. The words just pour from my mouth as if being coaxed out by the devil himself.

I don't have a tattoo. I've never had a desire to get one, and my mother would castrate me and feed me my own testicles if I even *thought* of getting one. Timmy, on the other hand, has plenty. His pale arms are covered in them. Everything from Green Day lyrics to Radioactive Man from *The Simpsons*. His body is a journal of his young life, written in faded greenish-black ink. "I got my first tattoo when I was fourteen. I didn't even think about it. That's the best kind of tattoo," Timmy tells me. I don't know if I'm going insane or just completely bored, but getting an impromptu tattoo sounds like the perfect cure for all of my tour troubles. And what kind of rock star doesn't have one? "I'll be back in a bit, Timmy. I'm getting a tattoo."

"So, you're saying you want a skull?" the dude says, holding a tattoo gun in one hand and a Marlboro in the other. "Yes, a skull. A menacing skull. On the inside of my arm. But I don't have a lot of time. My tour manager is waiting back at Burger King." This guy is a monster. Long black hair, stubbly face, and a frigid stare. He probably works out more than he sleeps. And his body is just drenched in ink. Muscular, frightening, joyless. He scares the shit out of me. I can't even make sense of his tattoos because they all run together to form one big black tattoo. Now, this is my first experience with tattooing. My first time in a tattoo parlor. And maybe this guy assumed I was experienced because I walked in there with such confidence and poise. Or stupidity, whatever you want to call it. He sucks on the cigarette once more, ashes it out, and gets to work. No dialogue, no nothing. First, he dips his tattoo gun into a little plastic cap filled with black ink, and then he reaches over to a radio and pushes the power button. The explosive roar of metal. Screaming guitars and human suffering. The darkest, most evil music I've ever experienced. The inspiration for this fucking evil tattoo.

Now comes intense, ceaseless, stinging pain. Tattoo torture. I look at the beast's face, and he's enjoying the *fuck* out of this right now. Like Ed Gein sawing the skin off of his victims to make belts and little skin hats. "It hurts. You have to stop. You have to stop, sir," I tell him, panicked. But the gun is too loud, and he also just chooses to ignore me. "Sir, you have to stop," I say again. "I can't stop," he says. "It has begun." Before I know it, my arm is bloody and black. And there you have it. A skull tattoo. It's bigger than I had imagined. A *lot* bigger. I wish I would have been more specific on the size. No one will look at me the same ever again. "That'll be $200. Cash." I have to go to the ATM. He can sense that, so he points out the door. "There's an

ATM across the street at Taffy's Grill." My arm is throbbing in pain. A new kind of pain, though. If you don't have a tattoo, you don't know what it's like. Just imagine if a doctor gave you a flu shot, but instead of pulling the needle out of you, he dragged it through your skin like a knife for a solid half hour. I'm lightheaded, stumbling a bit. "Across the street?" I ask, even though I know what he said. He nods and pulls a fresh cigarette out from the pack.

The ATM at Taffy's Grill is covered in band stickers. Touring bands must make this mistake all the time. You're on tour, you're waiting for a show that may not even happen, and you're bored. So you park your van at Burger King, eat shitty food, and then walk over to the nearby tattoo parlor to get some more meaningless markings on your body. After you're done being professionally defaced by a guy who looks like he's been behind bars for most of his adult life, you realize you don't have any money. So strange . . . a musician without any money? The prisoner who ruined your skin directs you to the nearest ATM, and you withdraw two hundred bucks from the checking account you share with your girlfriend. And before you walk away, you slap your band's logo on the side of the ATM so that some other poor sap can check out your music later on the internet. It's sad. It's pathetic. And I'm now a part of the cycle as I slap my own stupid adhesive next to one that says JIZZ HELMET.

We are all losers. The Loser Club.

As I'm leaving the restaurant, the young lady working the cash register stares at my arm like it's gushing blood or something. Oh, that's right. I forgot. It *is*. I gaze downward into my tattoo wounds, and blood is running out of every gash. It's almost like a Halloween store prop at this point. Almost a laughable amount of blood. And I'm laughing because I'm losing consciousness. My vision is hazy. No, I'm fine. No, it's okay. I wave off a young couple who approaches me. I'm fine. Yes, thank you. All good here. Thanks. The new tile floor is soaked. Oh, God. I repainted the place red. This is not good. I need to sit down. I need to go back there and pay him, though. But I need to sit down.

The walls are closing in on me. The sound of an air horn or something far away and dull. Tiny bursts of white light dance in my eyes like fireflies. The girl behind the counter is saying something, but I can't hear it because my ears are shutting down, closing up shop. I'm a little teapot. Short and stout. This is my handle. This is my.

Spout.

"Nick, this is Doctor Alan. Are you with us?"

I can't see anything yet, but I can hear a man's voice, and I can smell his deodorant and mint gum. I can hear the sounds of beeping and shoes walking. I can feel something stuck in my arm, and when I swat at it, a chalky glove grabs my hand. "We don't want you pulling that IV out, okay bud?" I can see him now. He's older, with a white goatee and a handsome face. "Did I pass out?" I ask rhetorically. "Do we have a show?" "I don't know, bud. You passed out at a restaurant and hit your head, but you're going to be okay, and your friends are here." He rubs my head like my mom would do.

I almost just want to stay here for the rest of the tour and have this older man take care of me like a panda bear. Timmy steps forward and shakes his head. "Duuuuuuuuude," he says, laughing a little. "I can't believe you passed out." I cock my head to the side, and Rich is sitting in a chair next to my bed. "You're an idiot, dude," he says.

We don't play a show that night. Ronnie lies to me and says it's because I passed out, but I look at his phone while he is stuffing his face with fast food and see the text messages from our touring company saying a show hadn't been booked. It's a big clusterfuck of time-sucking stupidity. The whole goddamn tour. But the upside is, when my mother finds out, she cries and cries and cries and blames herself for letting me go on tour and getting the tattoo and passing out and yada yada yada. She feels so bad that she books us a hotel. With two big beds. So we won't have to spoon each other. We rent four porno movies on pay-per-view for $19.99 a pop, watch them all back to back, and the next morning, we tell the concierge that it must have been a mistake and we get them all taken off the bill. I even steal a pillowcase and fill it with mini shampoo bottles so that I can bathe on the road.

"Good-night, ladies and gentlemen. I'm Nicholas Megalis." *Bam.* Rich slams into a dizzying guitar solo, and Timmy washes out the sound with his cymbals. I stand up on my piano and kick it off the stage. The only four people in the crowd clap unenthusiastically for a few seconds, and I take a bow. The best show of the tour so far. Backstage, Timmy wipes his face off with a towel as Rich puts his guitar gently back in its case. "I love you guys," I say to my friends. Rich doesn't look up, but he says it back to me. And Timmy gives me a bear hug. A good, solid hug. He sniffs at me. "What's that smell, dude?" I don't know what he's talking about. I mean, I can smell it, sort of. But barely. Anyway, never mind that. I can feel the power tonight. The world isn't so bad. I'm in a band with my best friends, and we just blew the pants off a few people. And that's fucking awesome. Even if no one knows who I am. Even if it's just a glorified hobby of mine. I feel like a legend. A hero. I am Nicholas Megalis, and I am rock 'n' roll.

The next morning, as the golden sun rises above our shared room at the Super 8 motel in the beautiful city of Los Angeles, California, the smell of my massively infected tattoo is so bad that it wakes up my entire band.

FOOTBALL SUCKS

"Touchdowwwwwwwwn Steeeeeeelersssssssssss!!!!!"

My old man jumps to his feet and screams at the top of his lungs, waving a little yellow towel in the air like an idiot. I look up from the book I'm reading. I'm on Chapter 6 of *The Mineral Manual*. I'm at the part where they talk about sphalerite and how it's combined with copper to make brass. You know, superthrilling stuff for a twelve-year-old boy.

"Nicky, did you see that? Bettis is the king! Look at him go!" my dad screams at me. "Yeah, Dad. Please," I say, completely shutting him down. My dad is on year twelve of trying to get me remotely interested in sports. We've gone through everything you possibly can do with a ball. Always pushing gently, but never forcing me into it. "Maybe you and I can throw the football outside when the game's over?" he asks me. It's the last thing on the planet I would ever want to do, aside from maybe watch paint dry or sit in a chair facing the wall. I can see the disappointment in his sad smile. He wants a real son. Not some book-reading pansy. Nah, that's not it at all. He's not like that.

SPHALERITE

He's an artist, but he's also this star athlete who played football in high school, and he talks about it constantly. A husky little Greek tank of a man. Like a Mediterranean bull. If my dad puts on a blazer and some sunglasses, he could pass for a mobster. He's had to "handle a few things" in his lifetime. Never put a hit on anybody, but he's picked up a crowbar or two.

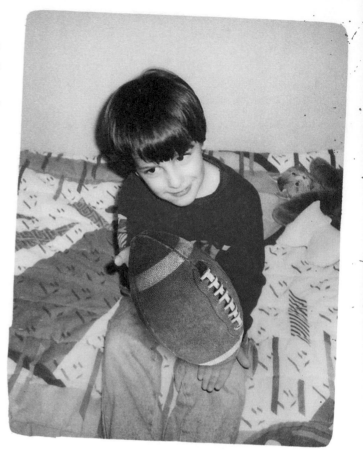

"Nicky, I'll show you how to kick a field goal," my dad says, his eyes widening as he excites himself. Okay, fine. You've annoyed me enough. I toss my book onto the couch and join him in our backyard for some pigskin. I couldn't be less enthusiastic. I'm dragging my feet, my head tilted back toward the ceiling, exhaling heavily. "Why do I have to play football, Dad? I draw. I ride my bike. I'm in Spanish club." I'm making myself sound like a loser right now. *Spanish club.* Are you kidding? Me, the girl with Tourette's, and the kid with halitosis are all learning how to ask for directions and name our favorite colors. *That's* an example of me being *active*? "Get your butt over there and catch this long pass!" my dad says, pointing toward the far end of our backyard. Ugh. I'll try to run, I guess. My legs might as well be string cheese. My arms dangle at my sides as I awkwardly jog away from my dad.

I look back and squint through the bright midday sun. My dad is standing there, probably wishing I hadn't been born. I'm a sad excuse for a boy. But then again, who the hell is he, Don Shula? Does my dad really think he's coaching me to be this next big football genius? He's an illustrator for God's sake. A commercial director! He was a football player in *high school.* That was nearly *thirty years ago.* Let's see him try to throw this pass. Let's see what he's worth. *Whoosh.* The ball is airborne. And it's coming at me fast. Damn . . . "You got it!" Dad yells from across the lawn. I wince, and I hear the ball land somewhere nearby in the grass. I couldn't see the pass because I was shielding

my face like the man had just thrown an explosive. "Nicky, don't be scared. Throw it back. Let's try it again," he says. "Dad, I'm done! I want to go read. This is stupid. I'm not into sports." I'm such a pussy. I'm frightened of a football. This is ludicrous. I just don't want to get hurt, but how bad could it be?

I pick the ball off the ground and stare at it like it's from another planet. I don't even know how to grip the thing. "Hold it along the stitching, Nicky. Then pull your arm back and throw it. Come on, you can do it!" Dad encourages me. So I throw it. *Smack*. It hits my little sister in the back of her head. "Sorry, Livvy!" I say. She's eight years old. She turns and stares menacingly from the driveway. Her long espresso hair hangs over her peace-sign T-shirt. But she's not keeping the peace today. "What the heck, Nick? Watch where you're throwing that! You don't even know how to play football!" Livvy barks at me. She clenches her fists and stomps away in her flip-flops.

Dad's got the ball again. "Look, I can teach you a trick that will help you catch a ball every time. When I was playing football in high school, I was pretty darn good, and the coach taught us to think of the ball as a roll of toilet paper. So when the ball's coming at you, just think of that. Pretend it's soft, and you won't be scared. And then you can focus on how to *catch* it!" my dad says. "You got this, Nicky. You got this." I'm not supremely confident today. I never like being forced to do anything. I like to do things on my own, and I only like to do things I'm good at.

My dad winds his arm up and nods at me from across our makeshift football field. The intensity in this man's face is unbelievable. He thinks he's about to throw a pass in a football movie. The ball leaves his arm and sails toward my face in an arc. I could puss out and cover my face again, but I have a feeling it'll knock my glasses right off my face if I do that. And my dad might let me finish *The Mineral Manual* if I just catch it. Toilet paper. Toilet paper. Toilet paper. I'm saying it over and over in my head. Just then, the ball morphs into a white, cottony roll of ass-wiping material. It lands beautifully into the cradle I've made with my arms. I clench it tightly against my chest. I've done it! Unreal. I finally caught a football. I think my dick grew three sizes with that catch. I'm finally a *man*.

My dad runs at me full speed and picks me up. He spins me around as if we're in a dream. A dream that *he's* having. I don't know if he's prouder of me or of himself for that whole "football as toilet paper" motivational speech. "You're the next great American receiver!" my dad proclaims loudly to the whole neighborhood. I'm sure if our neighbors had witnessed the mediocrity of that pass and reception, they would have been disgusted. But I'm gonna let Dad have his moment.

Go ahead, spin me around and pretend I'm your perfect football son. You fucking weirdo.

That night, my dad takes me, my brother, and my sister out for ice cream. It wasn't my idea. I don't crave ice cream as much as I crave sardines. Yeah, I'm that kind of kid. The kid who eats weird shit. While my friends are trading candy, I'm eyeballing the salted fish. I'm a freak, what can I say? My mom buys me capers, and I down *jarfuls* at a time. We're driving down Mill Road, on our way to the Dairy Queen. My little brother, a four-year-old screwball with a crooked tooth in the very front of his smile and permanent dirt stains on his face, slaps his pudgy legs in time to the song on the radio. It's Shania Twain's "Man! I Feel Like a Woman." My mother sits shotgun, singing tunelessly out the window at all of our neighbors because she doesn't give a flying fuck. "I'm the best singer in the world. You got your voice from me!" she says. But she knows very well that the sounds coming out of her mouth could only be described as the pained shrieking of a dying marine animal. My sister is writing in her diary. It's covered in peace signs and sunglasses and smiley faces and other stuff that eight-year-old girls draw on the cover of their diary to keep their brothers the hell out of it.

We sit in the far corner at the front of the store. Our spot. The ice cream melts down onto my football-playing hands while my dad brags to the kid mopping the floor at Dairy Queen. The long-haired acne-ridden employee is miserable enough scrubbing scuff marks off the floor, and on top of that he has to listen to my old man tell him how good his son is at football. "He's good. He's got a good arm. Good eye. I'm telling you, remember this face." Dad points to my face. I'm mortified. The kid doesn't stop mopping, and he just looks up at me and smiles, showing his braces. Both of us are embarrassed to have to even look at each other. It's an unnecessary exchange.

That night, on the way home from ice cream, my dad stops at the grocery store and picks me up a gigantic box of football cards as we all wait in the car. He opens the sliding van door and tosses the box onto my lap. "Here you go. Study these guys!

These are the greatest of the greats. There are five hundred cards in this box. The guy said these are the best cards he's got!" my dad says, pumped up on ice cream and his own natural insanity. In five hours I have become my dad's star athlete son based on a single fluke catch. I open the plastic wrapping and dig through the box. Names I've never seen before. Ridiculous mustaches and afros. Offset type and smudged ink. Lost almost-coulda-been football heroes on sale in a pack of five hundred cards for $9.99. "Dad, all of these cards are from 1982," I say from the backseat. "Yeah, Nicky. Of course. That's fine. The rules are still the same! These guys are the best. The best from 1982!" He turns his head and shouts at me, almost wrecking our van into an oncoming bus. "Watch the road, you Greek idiot!" my mom says as she smacks my dad in the back of his huge Greek head.

My dad laughs it off. Because almost killing your entire family is a joke.

I spend hours combing over these '80s trading cards from the comfort of my bunk bed. The red caterpillar-like mustache of one quarterback intrigues me. The tiny black type on the back of the card is nearly totally faded. His stats might as well be the stock exchange. It's a foreign language to me. All the abbreviations, the numbers

. . . I just like the color of his mustache. And I like the way the card feels. I've always had a thing for paper. The smell of it. The way it feels between my fingers. I think it's half the reason I like to read books. It's some obsessive-compulsive thing that I can't explain without sounding absolutely nuts. I can dig my nose into a newspaper and just inhale it. That's my cocaine.

"Nicky." Dad knocks on my door and invites himself in. "I've got a big surprise for this Sunday. You wanna know what it is?" He's wearing a hat that belongs to my sister. On one of his usual anxiety-fueled rampages to find a hat, he grabbed a random one and didn't notice that it sits on just the tip of his head. And also that it has a ladybug pattern on it and a cord strap. "Nicky, do you wanna know the surprise?" "No, Dad, I don't. Because a surprise is a surprise. That's why it's called a surprise. Dad, you don't tell someone what the surprise is," I inform him, annoyed. "Okay! See you on Sunday for the football game," he says as he almost skips out of my room. I don't know if he purposefully ruined the surprise to be a dick or if he literally didn't realize it. But he ruined it. I jump down from the bed and catch him in the hallway. "Dad, what game?" I ask. "Oh, we're going to see the Steelers play the 49ers. My buddy John invited us. He's bringing his son too. We have a loge! It's a private box where they feed you and bring you beers . . . I mean, sodas and sub sandwiches and all kinds of stuff. And you watch the game! You'll get to see the pros do it. Take notes. You're the next legendary quarterback, I have a feeling."

The kickoff. The muted cheers of sixty-five thousand fans at Heinz Field. Thick Pittsburgh accents screaming out "Fuck yeah!" and "Hell fucking yeah!" This is Steelers Nation, a world that I have decidedly not participated in for my entire life. Tens of thousands of little yellow "Terrible Towels" waving in the air to root for the home team. I'm eating a hot dog smothered in Pittsburgh's famous ketchup. My dad sips on a beer with his buddy John. "My boy is gonna be the next Johnny Unitas," Dad boasts with beer breath. "Is that right? You gotta put some meat on your bones first, Nick!" John chuckles, his belly jiggling up and down and making me want to throw up. John has the thickest Pittsburgh accent of all. Every sentence is coated with a nasty regional dialect that I still fight off to this very day. But it's ingrained in me, carved into my tongue like an ancient language. John smacks my arm. The brute. I'd rather be on my couch reading about stalagmites, **but here I am, eating a hot dog in a glass box with the dumbest people I've ever met.**

Now, my dad's no fool. He's probably studying these people, secretly casting them for a weird movie in his head. He can do anybody's accent. Anybody. From Sylvester Stallone to the guy serving peanuts, my old man has a knack for perfect mimicry. It's one of his many blessings. And he gets it from his mom, a tiny Greek woman who used to come home from her job at the hospital, where she folded laundry for two dollars an hour, stand in the kitchen with her arms crossed, and imitate her asshole boss *perfectly*.

I'm not paying attention to the game. I'm too distracted by John's son, Danny. Danny's a big boy. His Steelers jersey is mustard-stained and ill-fitting. It hangs off of his conical nipples, which I can't stop staring at. Big, pointy breasts. His hair is spiked and dyed blond just on the tips. He's missing an adult tooth in the front of his mouth, and when he speaks, his breath is warm with hot dog musk. "I'm gonna play for the Stillers," he says in that horrible accent. "I'm gunna get myself a model wife and pork her brains aut." His arms double-fist hot dogs into his mouth as he lays out his plan for NFL domination. "When I get my first Super Bowl ring, I'm gunna pork my wife every night and put the ring up inside her." I can't believe what he's saying. Not only am I offended, but I'm deeply confused as to why you'd ever want to put your Super Bowl ring inside a woman's vagina.

it makes no sense to me.

"Why don't you guys go and play some one-on-one?" My dad says to Danny and me. "Yeah, boys, go aut and get some runs in!" John chimes in, taking another sip of his beer. Before I can say a word, Danny grabs my arm and yanks my body hard. "Let's go, dude!" he says. Danny brought his own autographed football. His dad knows some of the players, and somebody high up owed him a favor. It's covered in black Sharpie. Names I can't decipher. As we leave the room and walk down the carpeted hallway toward the parking garage, Danny tells me all about his favorite players and which of them has the biggest dick. "I think Bettis has a tiny dick. A big black guy like that probably has a tiny dick." "Danny, I don't know about that. I heard black guys have big dicks," I argue. "In fact, I've seen pictures of black guys, and their dicks are all big." Danny shrugs and tosses me the ball. I barely catch it. We're standing in the middle of an upper-level parking garage where all the Steelers players park their expensive cars. License plates with yellow and gold trim all over. The distant sound of cheering and the announcer's voice booming in echoes. ". . . to the thirty five-five-ive-ive . . .

FOOTBA

to the thirty-thirty-irty-irty . . ." "Think fast!" Danny says as he chucks the ball full force at me. I turn my head just in time to grab the ball out of the air. But the impact is hard. This kid is a nightmare. He's one of those kids with major pent-up aggression that's just brewing inside of him and at any moment could explode like Mount Peleé. "Ha! You pussy. You don't catch like that! Your dad said you could catch! You caught like a pussy!" Danny torments me. I wish my dad wouldn't have opened his stupid mouth and told John that I could play, because now I have this image to maintain. An image that isn't even fucking real. "Come at me. Come at me, you pussy!" Danny taunts, spreading his fat legs and fat arms to protect an imaginary end zone. I get this feeling inside me that I've only had a few times in my life. This fucking rush of adrenaline. I've never done crack, but I imagine it's akin to a hit off the ol' crack pipe. My heart is burning, goose bumps rush over my arms, and this fiery, fucked-up anger takes over my brain. I'm not even me anymore. I'm someone else. A killer. A maniac. A football *legend*. I push off the ground and launch myself at Danny. He's only about three yards from me, so I arrive at my destination quickly. Why I thought my tiny, scrawny body would magically be able to knock Danny over and score a touchdown, I don't know. My face hits Danny's tits like a brick wall. I collide with this kid like you wouldn't believe. My nose swells with pain, and blood pours out of both nostrils like a vermilion waterfall. Not just a few drops. Ribbons of thick scarlet liquid cascade down my face and onto Danny's football, coating his prized autographs like paint. "Fucccccccccckkkkkk!" Danny moans, as he lifts his arms up and steps away from the scene. "You ruined my football, you pussy! You ruined my football!" I panic and start to run the opposite way to find the nearest bathroom. I back into a car, and the alarm goes off. My blood is spurting onto the doors like I'm a lawn sprinkler. The license plate says BETTIS.

I am proud to hold the record for Shortest Football Career. The Terrible Towel that I used to stop my nose from bleeding is on display in the Football Hall of Fame in Canton, Ohio, with a gold placard underneath that says "Nicholas Megalis, Pussy." The blood is blackened now, but it still serves as a constant reminder to all visitors that kids like me should probably just stay home on the couch and read *The Mineral Manual*. Oh, and I still have my football cards. Most of them, anyway. I googled the guy with the caterpillar mustache, and he's a registered sex offender.

↓

LL SUCKS.

THERE IS ALWAYS A DARREN

The apartment smells like plastic-bottle vodka.

You know the stuff. The kind that burns holes through styrofoam and your esophagus. The tiny meows of dying kittens filter through a box fan that sits in the open door. My Haitian roommate is on the phone, screaming at someone in Creole.

She speaks with her hands. And she breaks things with them. Like the remote control to the television I purchased for us. Or the statue of a dog that I had made in remembrance of my dear pug that overdosed on chocolate cake. While she bickers with her mother, she grabs hold of anything and everything in sight. Books, hairbrushes, boxes of cereal. Then just as quickly as it started, the fight is over.

I live with two other people. This is my first proper New York City apartment, and I'm lucky enough to share it with two of the most impossible human beings I've ever met. The twenty-six-year-old Haitian telemarketer with a short fuse named Johanne and a twenty-two-year-old bodybuilder slash absolute moron named Darren. I'm nineteen, and apparently a musician. I'm trying my best. Cut me a break.

I responded to a Craigslist ad looking for a roommate—"$400 a month. No pets."—yet here we are, my steroid-bloated roommate and myself, holding kittens in our hands. Dying and/or dead kittens in our shaking hands. Darren's an idiot. An actual idiot. And I guess I am too. Shit, we all are.

It's July and 106 degrees. The guy on the TV says so. I can't quite see his little meteorologist face because there's a line of static cutting through him. I bend the wire hanger to adjust the picture. Yeah, it's one of those setups. Ghetto-rigged. The guy's face warps and twists into infinite fields of pixelated color. Outside, the streets are filled with assholes, and the assholes are filled with shit. My mom sent me a check a week ago, and I already blew it on Chinese food and cigarettes. I woke up this morning to Darren and the telemarketer having an explosive fight in our living room. She threw a plate with an etching of a naked lady that had belonged to his grandfather, and it exploded against our dirty walls. He tried to grab her throat, but she spit on him. What a wonderful group of people.

Three p.m. and nowhere to be. Darren's sister, Alex, is sitting in a chair, smoking weed out of an open window in our teeny kitchen. Like Darren, she, too, is an idiot. I guess it runs in the family. She's gorgeous, though. Stunning. But so, so, so incredibly stupid. "Darren, you have to hydrate them. Put the needle into their stomach," she says, turning to face us. Pot smoke rolls out from an opening in her puffy lips.

Let me back up a little. I'm getting ahead of myself because I'm so upset. My roommate was working out one afternoon, doing chin-ups on a workout bar that's wedged between the frame of his bedroom door, when he got a call from his sister, a veterinarian's assistant on Long Island. She was probably stoned at work, screwing up paperwork for rich people's prized pets. Darren had just finished ripping from a huge bong that looked like a sword. "I spent eight hundred bucks on this fucker. It's from *Lord of the Rings*," he once bragged to me. I couldn't believe anyone on this earth would pay for it. But alas, there is Darren.

There is *always* a Darren.

I listened to their phone call over speakerphone from my inflatable bed. I sit on it most of the day, recording my voice into a laptop and playing acoustic guitar, writing drunken songs about my roommates and how much I hate them. The simple siblings conversed, both high out of their minds in different settings. One is high in a professional environment. The other, in a dirty apartment in Bed-Stuy, sweaty, and full of testosterone and bad decisions.

Here is how the call went:

ALEX: Darren, what's up? I need you to do me a favor. I'm selling some cats, and I need you to take care of them for a few weeks until we can find a home.

DARREN: Sure, Sis. Sounds dope. How old are they? You think you can pay me?

ALEX: I dunno, a day old? Two days? They're the size of a pack of gum. I can pay you in weed.

DARREN: Okay, Sis. Come by with a dime bag and the kittens. I'm home with my roommate Nicholas. He's cool sometimes.

ALEX: Sweet, see you soon.

When Alex arrives with the box of kittens, I'm just getting back from a trip to the grocery store to replenish my bologna and ketchup supplies. I'm a gourmet chef, look at me. Ramen noodles too. Don't get me started. Alex is holding a cardboard box at her breasts, and I try not to stare down her shirt. I peek inside. The box, not the shirt. Nestled into a baby blanket are four of the most malnourished looking animals I've ever seen in my life. It's just sadness. One of the kittens is shaking. Literally convulsing. Another is trying to cry out, presumably for its mother, but nothing comes out of its tiny mouth but air. None of them have their eyes open. It's just the worst.

I am now furious that I didn't intervene sooner. This was a major mistake. A stoned decision. A transaction between two biologically related simpletons who should absolutely not be handling animals in any capacity. "Alex, set the box down on the couch. Or give it to Nicholas." Alex tries to hand me the box, but my arms are so weak. My entire body is so weak. I feel like I could throw up right here onto the heads of these innocent kittens. Who the fuck does this dude think he is? He can't take care of kittens! He can barely take care of himself.

"Take these. I'm gonna roll us a blunt."

Alex walks into the kitchen and pulls out a bag and some papers, turning our little apartment into a blunt factory. She sets her iPod down on the kitchen table and puts on some Bob Marley. I'm sick to my stomach, looking down into the box. I lower my shaking hand into the blanket to comfort one of the kittens, and it is stone cold. Hard as a rock. Jesus Christ, it's dead. One of the fucking kittens is already dead. Rigor mortis. "Alex, one of them is dead. . . ."

"Oh, I know." she says. "So sad. Just cover him up or something."

Fighting the onset of a colossal panic attack, I inhale deeply and cover the kitten with the end of the blanket. Darren sits down on the couch beside me, and Alex sits on the floor like a little kid. She licks the blunt and runs the flame of a Bic underneath to seal it. "This is good shit. You're gonna be fucking high," she laughs. But I'm not laughing. How could I?

The brother and sister smoke the weed and watch stolen cable on our tiny TV. I refuse to partake. I'm too distraught to join them. Johanne has just left to spend the week in Haiti, thank God. Her door is locked. We each have a lock on our bedroom door. But when I went back home to visit family recently, Darren had managed to break into my room with a credit card and some elbow grease. So much for locks. When I confronted him, he laughed at me. "Dude, I needed to borrow some deodorant. I was fresh out." That was his brilliant excuse. I can't deal.

I'm in hell right now. These people are insane. I have to save these kittens. I have to call someone. But who do you call? The vet? This girl is the veterinarian's assistant, for God's sake!

"Let me show you guys how to hydrate them," Alex says, exhaling the thick smoke.

Hydrate?

Alex then proceeds to pull a plastic IV drip bag and needle from her purse. Like the shit you see in hospitals. She gently lifts a half-dead kitten from the box and flips it over on its back. I can feel myself teetering on the verge of unconsciousness. I struggle to not pass the fuck out. "You find the soft spot and you just prick it with this needle and hold the bag up until you can see the drip. It's sugar water or something. I can't really remember." She can't really remember what's in the bag because when the veterinarian told her, she was baked like a cake. Jesus Christ.

The needle is in. I can't breathe. She hands Darren the drip bag, and he holds it up for a second and then complains that his arm is tired. The guy who spends five hours a day exercising his biceps has a weak arm. Right. He's just too lazy and stoned to do it, so he grabs a hammer and a nail from our house toolkit and tacks the bag up on the living room wall. Like some morbid decoration. Our apartment has now turned into an emergency room for small animals. Fucking fantastic.

"Do you guys think the smoke bothers their lungs?" I ask worriedly. Alex laughs. Girl think's I'm joking. Darren doesn't even answer; his eyes are fixed on the television set. *Jeopardy!* is on, but I can't even see the categories through the static. Only one of the three roommates has actual income, and she sure as hell won't chip in for a cable package so that me and this meathead can watch *Jeopardy!*. I am lazy. I am unfocused. I am unemployed. I need to get my shit together, and fast.

We all take turns "hydrating" the kittens. I am having an out-of-body experience now as I stick another tiny ball of fur with an oversized metal syringe. There is no way on God's green earth that this is the proper way to nourish them, but I am so scared, I can't even react. I don't know a whole lot about cats, but I imagine puncturing something's stomach with a rusty needle is probably not the best way to give it a drink.

I can't handle this anymore. I'm absolutely done.

I leap off the couch with a kitten in my hand and reach over and grab the bag off the wall. I yank so hard, the bag rips open, spilling "sugar water or something" out onto our stained carpet that hasn't been cleaned since the Kennedy administration. "What the fuck are you doing, Nicholas?" Darren says, sobering up. He puts his cat in Alex's free hand. She now is holding two dying kittens. It's a miserable sight. They hang limply over her open palms, too fragile to hold their heads up. He stands face-to-face with me. His sweaty shoulder muscles glisten in the light of the TV. "This is insane! We have to do something!" I feel my panic attack brewing like a summer storm. I am so angry, I want to punch the both of them, but I'm not a strong guy, so I'll have to use my words.

"Calm down, dude! My sister is a vet, bro!" Darren snaps. His heavy Long Island accent is so irritating, especially right now. I want to slug him in his muscular throat. I want to knock him on his muscular ass. I want to break his beautiful, muscular arms. I breathe in deep and prepare to unleash a verbal blow like he's never been dealt before. I have a big mouth. I wind up my tongue like a pitcher winds up the ball.

And here . . . we . . . go.

"First off, she's not a veterinarian. She's a vet's *assistant*. She doesn't have the brain cells to be a veterinarian, and she's going to get fucking fired when she comes in on Monday morning because I'm reporting her the second I walk out this door. Secondly, you have absolutely *zero* business handling anything with a pulse because you're a barbarian. You walk around here and flex and steal my deodorant, which is unsanitary and disgusting and you smoke weed all day because you haven't developed your brain enough to even *know* to do anything else. Back the fuck away from that box. I am taking all of these kittens, and if you have a problem with it you can punch me in the face right now because I don't give a flying fuck about either of you."

BOOM. The punch is so hard, so mighty, I don't even feel the hit. It's not until an hour or so later, when I am nursing a black eye on the roof of my apartment building in the rain, that I can fully grasp the impact. I can feel my heartbeat in my face. It hurts. Like hell. The throbbing pain starts in my swollen eye socket and pitter-patters its way into my chin and down into my neck. Darren cold-cocked me into the next world. And that world is my apartment building's rooftop. The rain soaks my clothes and ruins my phone. I check to see what time it is, and the screen is soaked. I'll have to ask my mom for more money. Shit.

I look up into the blackness, into the storm. I could get struck by lightning right now, and I would die happy. At least I said something. My big mouth. Always my big mouth. Frozen peas now, onto my skin. That feels better, sort of. Frozen peas, I love you.

The kittens are all dead by midnight. Darren is drunk. the kittens are in a garbage bag by the door. Alex is gone. I wish I could have said good-bye to her breasts. Darren hands me a beer, and I take it. It's cold and tall, but it tastes like piss. All beer tastes like piss, but we pretend to enjoy it to fit in. "Sorry, bro. But you were being a little bitch," Darren says nonchalantly as he takes a sip. "I know, dude." I can't believe I am sharing a drink with the guy who whomped me. But I live with him. And I need a drink. Life is weird.

I don't know why he thought it was okay to play mother to a box of debilitated newborn cats. I don't know why he thought it was acceptable to break into my room and use my personal hygiene products. Nor do I know why he leaves used condoms in the toilet after his innumerable one-night stands. You can't flush them. It will clog the toilet. As we drink beers to the sound of the rain, I wonder why I am in New York City. I wonder every night. But somehow, when I wake up, I will love it again. And I will live another day in the strangest place on the face of the planet. More frozen peas on my eye. I look over at the spilled bag of "sugar water or something." It is a sad reminder of the wasted lives of those poor kittens that my beefcake roommate and his incompetent sister tried to raise as their own. Those kittens needed to be with their mother. It was too early to take them away. It makes me think of my own life. My own mother. I miss her so much. I finish my beer and step into my room. I lie on my back, sprawled out like Christ on my inflatable bed. I feel like I'm on a raft in the middle of the ocean. It hurts to blink. More frozen peas.

"Mom, I love you," I say onto her voicemail. "I miss you, and I can't wait to see you."

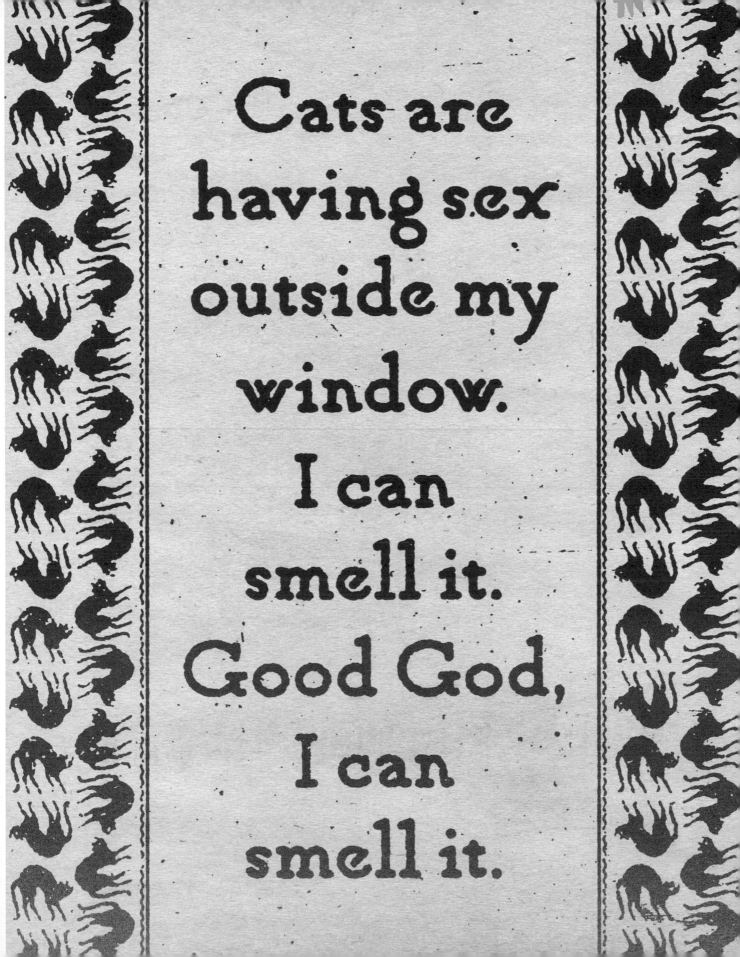

Cats are having sex outside my window. I can smell it. Good God, I can smell it.

AIN'T NOBODY IN NORTH CAROLINA WHO KNOWS BLOWING SHIT UP BETTER THAN YOU

"No touchin' things," the old woman says like some decrepit lifeguard as I inspect a box of rockets. She's eyeing us from across the store and smoking. Always smoking. You know, one lit cigarette in a fireworks store is a stupid mistake. Two cigarettes is pushing your luck. And a whole pack is a goddamn death wish.

"Oh, sorry about that. Nicky, watch out," my dad says, appeasing her. Another Megalis trick: pacifying people immediately so that you ultimately get what you want. "Just don't touch anything. Let's get out of here," he whispers as I shove more and more brightly colored crap into my plastic basket. A yellow Post-it note taped to a shelf reads ANYTHING ON SHELF 2 FOR 1 in nearly illegible handwritten Sharpie.

Like a looter in some kind of riot, like a panicked civilian stockpiling canned food and household items in the midst of a global meltdown, I shove "100 shot"-this and "fiery fountain"-that into my personal shopping basket like a little fucking lunatic. I'm a prepubescent Ted Kaczynski, minus the rambling manifesto. My dad shakes his head in disbelief as his psychotic son piles on the explosives. "What, are you planning to blow up the planet?" dad jokes. "Put some of that crap back, Nick. You can't buy the whole store."

But it's too late. I'm delirious. High off the stench of black powder and cardboard filling. The room shrinks down to the size of a peanut shell. It's just me and my fireworks in a twisted *Fear and Loathing* sort of nightmare. A meandering, serpentine shelf, piled as high as heaven with paper tanks and plastic-tipped missiles, circles around me forever and ever and ever as I choke on my own excited spit. A Roman candle blossoms open, and from the plumes of rainbow-colored smoke emerges a rattlesnake with a cigarette in its mouth and spiky red hair. Its face, feminine but withered. The snake half hisses, half talks at me: "No touching thingsssss." I keep loading my basket, but the basket keeps getting bigger. More fireworks! More, more, more! My dad's body has disappeared. It's just his voice, reverberating for miles and miles across the concrete walls of my peanut shell. "Nicky, let's go." But I won't go. I can't, not now. More, more, more! "Nicky! Enough!" My dad is no longer just a voice. His face is huge and dominating, his muscular arms are like trees swaying in a storm. He grabs for my fireworks and misses. I slap his arm, hard. "Don't you slap me," he says, even angrier. I can almost *see* his voice. It is red-tinged like the sun. I can feel the heat from his temper filling the peanut shell like truck exhaust. He grabs my arm and gives it a yank. His hand is dry and scratchy like a catcher's mitt. It burns my skin as he tugs harder. As he pulls, the snake laughs a little. I can't hear it, but I can smell the laughter. The Carolina sun is orange and soft. A polar bear on a ragged secondhand T-shirt opens his mouth, but its voice is not a bear's but my father's.

The peanut shell is getting smaller, hotter. A cat meows a thousand miles away. A ceiling fan wobbles and creaks almost musically. I grab hold of the winding metal shelves and clench for my life. I am anchored now. I am one with the fireworks dis-

play. I feel like an environmental activist who has chained himself to a tree to protest deforestation. I'm a goddamn fireworks martyr. Somehow, my basket has fallen to the floor. Except it isn't a floor. It's Cape Fear River, North Carolina's pride and joy. An alligator in a shitty plastic inner tube drinks Budweiser out of a can. My Reeboks don't penetrate the murky water. I stand as if on dirty glass. A school of striped bass sings a familiar song. Their tiny fish voices fill the peanut shell, making it warm again. They sound just like a barbershop quartet. *"Hold on to that shelf, Nick. Hold on for your life, Nick. Don't you ever stop, Nick. Hold on to that shelf!"* Both of my arms now are linked to the shelf. My dad will have to pry me off like a fried egg on a North Carolina windshield.

He's got my feet now. He's backing away, but I remain stuck to the shelves. I'm a human flagpole. My body is parallel with the floor. Both of my skinny arms grip the metal like carabiners. I am fastened with near-industrial strength. I am not fucking letting go. "Nicky, this is ridiculous. I'm going to count to three." The snake is laughing, the polar bear on the shirt is laughing, the alli-

gator is drinking a beer and laughing, the striped bass are dancing and singing and laughing. Everyone is laughing except Dad. "Three . . ." he says. The countdown has begun. The fuse has been lit. It fizzles and pops in anticipation. "Two . . ." My hands are wet with perspiration. Droplets of sweat roll down the lines in my palm and off my wrists and into the Cape Fear River floor. "Nicky, I'm not kidding, kidding, kidding, kidd, kid, ki, k . . .," Dad's voice echoes out into oblivion. I grip the metal even tighter. My ribs are aching. The ceiling fan creaks musically. It's a beautiful song:

In the summertime,
There's an Iris
That blooms blue and wild like you.
Do not pierce it, let it live and die,
My Carolina true

"One."

Dad pulls. Hard. I am one with the shelves. We live together, we die together. We stand together, we fall together. "Sir!" the old woman protests uselessly. She tried, but it is far past the point of stopping this disaster. No more tug of war. No more silliness. No more drippy, wacky cartoon peanut world. The shelves move with my body, away from the wall and toward the floor. Toward me. A reality check unlike any I've experienced in my eight years on this planet. KABOOM

First, my dad collapses and lands somewhere behind me, presumably in a pile of Warner Brothers sound effects, because it is the most ludicrous thing I have ever heard. Then it is my turn. My skinny little frame topples to the cold tile floor. I am bathed in metal racks and their respective products. The smell of sulfur is stronger than ever, because now it is in my hair. My lips and cheeks are dusted with gunpowder, and my elbows are jammed into the center of two identical faux birthday cakes that blow up when you light a wick coming out of a paper bride's ass. I look up at the wall and see the faint, dusty outlines of where shelves once stood like glorious towers. Now I am wearing them.

My dad lifts me from the rubble. "You okay?" he asks, brushing soot off my face. He looks like a firefighter. Even though he technically *caused* this tragedy, he is my hero. And I love him infinitely. "Yeah, I'm fine." My butt is a little sore, but I'm scared to tell him. "Nick, we have to clean this up. We have to get the hell out of here," he says under his breath. "Where's my basket?" I whisper back. It's all I care about. The basket that I loaded up with fireworks. It's gone. He doesn't care. He's just frantically picking up broken shit and shoving it into a pile. Cardboard mortar tubes are cracked in half. Cherry bombs pour out of their ripped packaging and onto the floor. My dad nervously kicks them under a shelf that *didn't* fall down.

The old woman appears between my dad and me like a smoky ghost and hands us both a broom. Well, one regular broom and another just the broom part with no handle. "I am so, so sorry. He's just obsessed with fireworks, and I tried to pull him off, and he just held on, and I guess I pulled too hard, but you know what? He's learned a lesson, and you just can't do that. It's wrong, and he knows it," he talks nervously at her expressionless, furrowed face. She lifts a skeleton arm to suck on her cigarette and walks away. "Sweep," she says, not looking back.

"$157.85."

My heart nearly calls it quits right then and there. It feels like hours between heartbeats. One hundred fifty-seven dollars and eighty-five cents. That's how much we owe this lady for those cardboard tubes that fell on the ground. Those stupid little things filled with black dirt that you light on fire.

ONE HUNDRED FIFTY-SEVEN BUCKS AND EIGHTY-FIVE CENTS.

I'm just a kid, and I honestly have no clue how to save, spend, or make money. But I can tell that's a lot of dough. I remember a phone call between my dad and some guy who hired him to be in a furniture commercial. My dad played a sofa. Literally, he had to act like he was a couch. His face was painted brown like a cushion, and he sounded like a Greek Archie Bunker. I couldn't hear the other side of the call, but I listened as my old man talked business. It bored the shit out of me for the most part, but my dad said something on that call that would stick with me forever. "Money is gasoline. We need it to move."

I watch my poor old dad reach into his pocket and pull out his wallet. It's a fat wallet. Not fat with money. Fat with receipts for small purchases. McDonald's coffees, mostly. He's a hoarder of useless paperwork. I wish I could pay for the mess we made, but I can't. I have no money. Not even a penny for good luck. Someone has to right these wrongs. And unless this ancient lizard of a woman accepts pocket lint and football cards, I can't foot the bill.

"Well, I'll be a dog's dick!" A man the size of a small truck squeezes into the store, wearing a red bandanna wrapped around his bald noggin and aviator sunglasses hanging from a T-shirt that says KABOOM FIREWORKS: THE BEST IN NORTH CAROLINA. He's about six feet tall, and his stomach six feet round. He's got as many teeth as I can count on one hand, minus my thumb. Chewing tobacco stains his chin and runs off down into the rolls of his neck, where they crystallize and remain for centuries as he clearly doesn't believe in the art of bathing.

My dad looks up from his sad wallet and adjusts his eyes onto the biggest boy in North Carolina. The guy is so enormous, it's hard to take him in with just one glance. You gotta *really* take him in. "Holy shit on a fuckin' dog's dick!" Big Boy spouts Southern-twanged profanities out of his tiny, toothless mouth as he moves toward us, one tree-trunk leg at a time. "Hey, buddy, do I know you?" my dad asks as Big Boy stops in his tracks and puts his huge arm onto his shoulder. "You're the goddamn couch!"

Oh, good God, this man recognizes my dad. From the furniture commercial. The one where my dad is in brown-face, playing a couch cushion. The old man smiles when he gets it. And Big Boy loses his goddamn *mind*. "Oh, my fuck! Oh, my fuck! It's him, Sandra, it's him!" Finally, we learn the old bag's name: Sandra. "I love that commercial, god*damn!*" Big Boy says as he squeezes my dad's shoulder, nearly crushing it. "It's always so nice to meet a fan! I can't believe they air those commercials down here. We're from Pittsburgh," Dad says, seething in pain from the loving embrace of his biggest fan, quite literally. "Sandra, you seen them commercials? This is the couch! This guy right here is the goddamn couch!" Sandra doesn't give a flying turd. She just lights another cig and breathes in deep.

"What the fuck are you doing down in North Carolina?" Big Boy asks. "Well, we're on vacation. And this is my son. He's got a baby brother back home and a little sister. Say hi, Nicky!" my dad says, pushing my arm a little. "Hi. I'm Nicholas," I say, keeping it formal. I always introduce myself as Nicholas to sound like I'm smart. And I'm a little embarrassed when my dad calls me Nicky. It makes me feel like a teenage girl or something. "Well, I hope you and Nicky are enjoying your fucking stay in North Carolina! Did y'all buy some of my fireworks today?" I can see the wheels spinning in my dad's eyes. And a slight smile, ever so slight, forming in the corners of his mouth. He's coming up with a plan. A natural performer, or a shyster, depending on how you spin it, my dad is a straight-up genius when it comes to social interaction. He can and *will* entertain your pants off, and leave with the keys to your Ferrari. He's the king of getting out of parking tickets. The Picasso of dealing with people.

"Yeah, you know, the thing is . . ." Here it comes. I can't wait to hear this. I'm practically quivering with anticipation. "The thing is, we came in here because of that sign outside."

There it is, there's the opening compliment. This is referred to as the *bait*. "The beautiful hand-painted one outside, was that your work?" Big Boy's face brightens up like a goddamn lightbulb. "Matter of fact, it most certainly was. My daddy was a sign painter, and his daddy before him. Now, I didn't join the family business, but I sure as hell inherited the skill," he boasts, moving around on his toes like an excited child. So proud. Just beaming with satisfaction. "Wow. And what a skill that is. I've never seen such care and precision in a sign before. My son is an artist, and so am I, so we just *had* to come in!" Big Boy is in my dad's net now, and he doesn't even know it. "Well, I appreciate that!

That fucking sign has been up there for twenty years. I repainted it last Tuesday!" I look up at my dad's face, and it's almost as if I can see straight into his brain. The gears moving, all the cogs clicking into place. "When we came in, we were so astonished by the selection. Nobody does fireworks like this anymore. *Nobody.* It's all Phantom and the big boys and no respect for the mom and pop. You guys do it right. You and your wife," Dad says. "That's exactly right! See, you get it, couch man. You get it! We've been selling fireworks for two decades right here. They wanted to kick us out, but we stood here when they brought the bulldozer. Nobody's taking my goddamn fireworks.

Not nobody, not no how!" Big Boy gets so worked up, he almost launches off the ground like he's a bottle rocket himself. "I wish I had someone like you on the Kaboom team! Hot damn, we would make a killing!" "If I didn't live in Pennsylvania, you'd have yourself a right-hand man!" my dad laughs. Sandra is smoking and listening. She occasionally nods or shakes her head, depending on the content of the particular dialogue. "See, now, my son knocked over a couple fireworks and, boy, he just feels so bad. We *both* feel so bad. We just wish there was something we could do. Your beautiful establishment and your hand-painted signage and all. It's just *gorgeous*."

This is the fork in the road. This is the part where the fat fish could either jump out of my dad's conversational net and swim away or get sautéed with a little garlic and oil and feed a family of five.

"Oh, shit! A couple fireworks fell off the shelf? Don't worry about it." I watch the words come out of his toothless, tobacco-stained mouth. His brown tongue knocks around his gums like a slug in mud. "It's a fuckin' honor to have the couch man in our store! Sandra, baby, would you be a princess and take a picture of us together?" Sandra doesn't miss a beat. She reaches into a particleboard cabinet and pulls out a disposable camera, and my dad and his biggest fan stand side by side. Together, the two men's bodies resemble the number 10. My dad is the 1 and Big Boy, of course, is 0. The flash of the cheap plastic bulb. The winding sound of the little gear. My dad has just gotten away with fireworks murder. And from his smiling glance down onto me, I know that he knows *exactly* what he's doing. "What a nice man, isn't he Nicky? What a good guy. What's your name, buddy?" Dad asks, reaching out for what will undoubtedly be the sweatiest, nastiest handshake in handshake history. "Buck. My name's Buck," Big Boy Buck says with massive pride. Sandra lights another cigarette and sits back down in her spot beneath the world's most dangerous ceiling fan.

Buck gives us a lifetime supply of explosives. For free. Okay, maybe not a *lifetime* supply, but enough to send me into a frenzy, and enough to drive my mother nuts for the next year and a half. He wrote off our damages like it never even happened, and even helped us load three overstuffed paper bags full of fireworks into the back of our crappy rental car. "Listen here, Tom. Whenever you're back in North Carolina, you give Bucky a call and we'll set you up with the best boom in town! The fucking best!" Bucky howls, slapping my dad on his back really, really hard. The slap echoes across the parking lot and into eternity. The slap heard around the world. The slap that marks the beginning of a lifelong friendship, one that blossomed out of my own childish behavior and my dad's lack of funds. My dad starts the car and rolls down the window. "Bucky, ain't nobody in North Carolina who knows blowing shit up better than you." Bucky laughs like a madman and spits a little tobacco into my dad's ear as we inch our way out of the parking lot and onto the open road. Godspeed, you morbidly obese fireworks impresario.

The sun is still hot, but soon it will give way to the Carolina stars.

AND TONIGHT, MY MOTHER WILL WATCH IN ABSOLUTE FUCKING TERROR AS I RUN AROUND SHIRTLESS, PLAYING WITH FIREWORKS THAT MY DAD CONNED OUT OF A MAN WITH NO TEETH.

ONE BUSINESS Week In LIL' ITALY

It's 4:00 in the afternoon. The door to our house at 120 Random Road is painted shut. Globs of almond-colored paint cake the doorknob and drip into the hinges. "Soooo...how are we getting into this dump?" Simon asks in his typical pissed-off way. Simon is two years older than me, a bone-thin Eastern European rock star with a short fuse and an obsession with tight pants. He drives a car that smells like incense, and he knows more about music than anyone I've ever met. A goddamn encyclopedia. He's my hero. He is coolness embodied. A scruffy outsider who gets all the girls but doesn't go with any of them. A pouty, strangely handsome misanthrope who smokes French cigarettes and spends hours tearing little holes into his clothes to make them look vintage.

We are standing on the front porch of our new home. Simon is slouched against the rotted wood paneling, checking his phone for text messages from various horny girls.

What a stud. I'm pretending to be cool too. My too-tight T-shirt reads 1987 WEEBLETOWN DOG SHOW. I wasn't born until 1989. What the hell do I know about 1987? I reach into my messenger bag and pull out a cigarette and a warm beer. My mom bought me this bag for Christmas. I doubt she predicted I would be using it to transport counterculture. It's the first week of June. I've just graduated from high school, and I'm headed nowhere. No college, no job, and no discernible skill set with any societal value. I'm 123 pounds. The thinnest I've been in years. At eighteen years old, I've adopted a vegan diet and an attitude problem. I look like a young David Bowie, except Greek. David Bowieopolous.

The night before my graduation ceremony, I shaved off all of my hair except for a patch right down the middle. White people, descendants of the bloodlines that raped and killed the Native Americans, refer to this hairstyle as the "mohawk." I walked into the kitchen, stood tall and proud, and my mother looked at my hair and said, "I hope they let you walk across the stage." She was, of course, concerned that the powers that be would take one look at my skinny frame and defiant hairdo and kick me out before I could grab a diploma. I was already playing with fire with my straight D-minuses. My worried teachers all rallied together and took turns at trying to "adjust" my education. But they weren't stupid. They knew I wasn't going to spend four years in yet *another* jail, pretending to pay attention while plotting a global takeover on the backs of my test papers. I wasn't cut out for a "traditional learning environment," as my principal politely put it. I'm sure in his head he was fantasizing an exquisitely brutal and thorough murder of me and my stupid face. "Nicholas, you'll excel no matter where you go," Mrs. Jonston told me. My art teacher. Of course. She was the only teacher who got it. Out of everybody, she was the one who actually got it. She was probably high as a fucking kite, though. "You can be a painter. You can be an author. You can make a movie. Whatever you do, you'll be successful." Strong words from a woman who didn't own one single piece of clothing that wasn't completely covered in cat hair. She always ate lunch by herself in the art room. One time I caught her eating paint. Eating *paint*. She begged me not to tell anyone. She told me it was an "experiment in becoming closer with the medium." Right...

I didn't rub shoulders with the jocks. I didn't quite fit in with the nerds. I was the ringmaster of my own Nicholas Megalis circus, and my teachers were just *frightened*. I once scored, directed, and cast a full theatrical production in the high school auditorium called *Homelessness: The Musical*. I charged ten dollars a pop and then turned around and gave all the money to a homeless man who lived in the woods behind our school. I had a top-secret sandwich ring in the cafeteria. A mafia-style lunch program that offered alternative options to the regular pizza and hamburgers. My guys hawked tuna salad with spicy brown mustard. Black forest ham on crunchy baguettes. Capers and cherry tomatoes. It was a black market deli. I was ambitious and loud. While barely passing any of my classes, I was laser-focused on what *I wanted to do*, and I was successful at it. Whatever it was. And my teachers were baffled. "You have all this drive, all this talent, and you're using the school paper to promote *Naked Tuesday*?" my guidance counselor asked incredulously. (Of course, he was referring to my made-up holiday that I promoted in the *Hallway Times*, a student-run rag that served better as a fish wrapper than as an actual source of news.) The ad for Naked Tuesday made it seem like an actual event. The loud, size-22 font asked that

"ALL STUDENTS ARRIVE TO SCHOOL COMPLETELY NAKED ON TUESDAY THE 18th."

With the help of my graphic designer partner-in-crime Tommy Waggler, we made a fake nude photo of our principal and used a smiley face to cover up his junk. I got the picture from a porn website, so I needed a pretty big smiley face to cover that monster up.

I met Simon on the first day of freshman year. I was fat, unpopular, and still getting decent grades. He was sitting by himself in the hallway, in front of his locker,

listening to music loudly through cheap plastic headphones, wearing a shirt that said TRUST NOBODY. Mind you, the shirt was handmade with a Sharpie. I assume he spent hours on this antisocial fashion commentary. The penmanship was outstanding. "I'm Nicholas," I said, reaching in to shake Simon's skinny hand. He looked like a model. Like one of those permanently bored-looking boys that you see in Urban Outfitters mailers. "What?" he said, removing one headphone and looking incredibly peeved. I was instantly attracted to his arrogance. He was an absolute wanker. No doubt. "I said, I'm Nicholas," I repeated, my hand still extended. Simon took a second to drink me in. My flabby arms, my soft face, my Hunchback of Notre Dame posture. "I'm Simon," he said, not very politely. Then he waited patiently for me to leave. "Okay, then. Well, nice to meet you, Simon," I said, walking away as he glared at me like I was a moron.

Simon and I would become awkward best friends over the course of the next four years. Simon had a license and I didn't, so he would be our getaway driver for all of our various teenage crimes. He taught me how to steal beer at Walmart by replacing all the cans in a twelve-pack of Coke with Pabst Blue Ribbon. We rode his uncle's Triumph motorcycle through the 'burbs at 3:00 in the morning with a baseball bat, smashing mailboxes and laughing like hyenas. I smoked grass with him and a Venezuelan exchange student on the roof of my parents' house and then watched them have sex in my dad's car. Simon drank a bottle of Jack Daniel's, puked on me, and drove his Toyota into a pond. We blamed it on a neighborhood drug dealer named Leylan. Leylan eventually found out and beat the shit out of Simon, and Simon retaliated by taking a dump on Leylan's grandmother's doorstep. Simon played guitar, and I played piano, and we knew an autistic kid who could slam the drums like no one's business, so we started a band called "The Dickwads" and played open mics. Really loud, miserable music. Just pure noise.

One time, we played at a neighborhood coffee shop, and the sixty-five-year-old owner approached us after the show and said, "This was the worst show we've ever had, and maybe the worst show there has ever been."

This was a crucial period of musical development for me. I was expressing myself and being rejected. And learning what not to do if I wanted any success.

I lost weight just by hanging around Simon. It rubbed off on me. He didn't eat meat, and he never touched fast food. His gorgeous, muscular father once told me in his thick, vaguely European accent,

 **"Simon doesn't eat shit. Because Simon isn't shit."**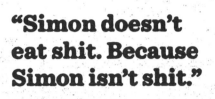

His whole family was beautiful. Perfect people. My family ate sloppy joes and drank lemonade and made fart jokes. Simon's family played water polo and collected World War II memorabilia and had a humidor in their basement. I never introduced any prospective girlfriends to Simon out of fear that he would steal them from me. He had done it before. Lexi Grant. The most beautiful girl in the tenth grade. A redhead with eyes the size of Texas and even bigger breasts. Simon was a senior, and Lexi was going out with me for two months before I caught the two of them tonguing in a car parked outside of *my house*. It's as if he had done it on purpose. Fuck, of *course* he did it on purpose. "I never want to see you again, dude. You're a fucking piece of shit," I said. And Simon drove off with Lexi. She called me that night to apologize, but I let it go to voicemail. I never talked to her again.

As I approached the last few months of twelfth grade, I still talked to Simon almost every day. He was busy with college, pretending to be a fine artist. The kid couldn't even hold a paintbrush properly, but he was having these big gallery showings and hobnobbing with art stars. I saw a photo of him in the newspaper wearing a fedora and smoking a clove cigarette, and on his shoulder was a blonde, photographed midlaugh. He looked like Gatsby. I started painting constantly to mirror Simon's new career. I invited Simon over after school one day to show off my "Fire Paintings." My parents bought me canvas, and I made crappy acrylic landscapes and then set them on fire. The charred remains were the finished works. "Dude, these are great. But you need more *soul*," Simon told me. "Yes, yes," I retorted. "More soul."

Then Simon dropped out of art school and traveled the country for a few months, fornicating with beautiful women and taking pretentious Polaroids of sunsets. It gave me time to focus on school, and Lord did I need it. I was treacherously close to failing the twelfth grade. My mom hired a math tutor; my dad bought me motivational books. Simon called me from New Mexico one night, whispered the words "Lil' Italy" into the phone, and hung up. It was cryptic, but I got it. We had been planning to rent a house together to consummate our bromance. And if I successfully graduated high school, like 90 percent of Americans do, I would be allowed to move in with him. My parents had already accepted that I wasn't going to college. My mother gave me an ultimatum: "Be successful or be a loser." And I accepted the challenge. I couldn't fathom draining my parents' savings account and wasting four years of precious time on this planet just for another piece of paper that could buy me a job that I would rather die than have.

I was carving out a path for myself. Sure, I was a little lost from time to time. But when I fell asleep at night, I knew in my heart that I was an artist. And I knew that I was going to be somebody.

Simon returned from his trip with long hair and a beard on the eve of my graduation, looking like a young Che Guevara. His worn-out jeans and motorcycle jacket. His smoky eyes and unlit cigarette to match. A sexy vagabond. A traveling man. "How did it go, Simon?" I asked him as we leaned up against his car in my driveway. He lit his cig, took a deep drag, and didn't even look at me as he said, "It was all I've ever dreamed of." Simon was a free man. No parents to make him study. No boss to nag him all day. No college professors forcing him to write stupid papers on stupid shit. My dad came out of the garage and said, "Hey, Simon! You wanna join us for movie night? We're renting *The Nutty Professor*." I was mortified. Simon peeled out and drove off into the sunset. That night, I gave myself a mohawk over the bathroom sink and packed my bags for Lil' Italy.

Lil' Italy is the part of Cleveland where all the real Italians go to drink cappuccino and play bocce. A hotspot for breathtaking pasta and gnarly gunfights, from the tippy-top of Mayfield Road all the way down to University Circle. My parents christened our move to Ohio with a stop in Lil' Italy. We ate pasta at Mama Santa's and drank coffee at Presti's Bakery. All through high school, I had dreamed of living in a house on Random Road. The houses were big and cheap. The backyards faced the train tracks, and when the trains passed through, it shook the houses from the foundation up. At the start of the street was a bar, at the end of the street was a bar. Random was bookended by booze. A tobacco shop was two blocks up the street on Mayfield, and parallel to that was a liquor store, where the senile owner never carded anybody. I had seen kids in there who were barely out of middle school, buying boxed wine. Place was a nuthouse. The owner looked like he was 150 years old, and he could barely pick up a bottle to put into a bag. You had to make sure you had a few hours to kill before you set foot in the liquor store because the old man would talk you into the fucking ground. "I had a dog with one leg: We called him Hopper. He fell into goddamn Lake Erie in 1967 and died right there. Drowned with that one leg. Hopper, his name was." "Oh, is that right?" I would ask, trying to grab my purchase and make a run for it. "I was a juice jerker in the Air Force. Mary Elisabeth Chatwater sent me a sugar report from Euclid when I was stationed in Eglin. She had tits like birthday balloons."

Simon found a house for a hundred bucks a month per roommate. For two bums with no jobs, a hundred clams a month was a pretty penny. "I sold some paintings. I think I have enough for at least half of the first month," Simon said, smoking and driving us to our new house. "We sign the lease, and then it's ours." My mom was an angel. She gave me an envelope with a heart drawn on it and kissed me and said, "This is for snacks, laundry, and girls. Don't let Simon know you have it. Guard it with your life." She never fully trusted him. She said he wasn't "raised right." Said he was "full of malarkey." Malarkey. I like that word.

"Welcome to your new home, boys," says a disembodied voice. We turn around to face a pudgy little guy with an obvious toupee and a stained button-down shirt, making his way up the steps to 120 Random. The landlord. He hands us each a piece of paper filled with a bunch of legal mumbo jumbo that Simon and I both don't want to read, and *can't* read because it's almost completely illegible after years of over-Xeroxing. "So, are your parents here to cosign?"

he asks, spit dripping down his fat chin. "No, we're both 18," I say. "I'm 20," Simon snaps, quickly correcting me. "Okay, then. Sign those and I'll be needing the $500 security deposit from both of you." Simon looks at me, and I look at Simon. Security deposit? "You have the security deposit, no?" Pudgy asks. "No, neither of us have it. You don't need it; we won't be fucking your house up. Just take our money and have a nice day," Simon says. He has spoken to authority like this in the past, but it's still just as shocking every single time he does it. Pudgy looks at Simon in disbelief, but he has no response. He nervously hands us both a blue pen, and we sign it, and the guy gets in his little poop-brown car and takes off. Unbelievable. "I ain't giving that guy *shit*," Simon says, reaching for the doorknob.

Inside our house, there is crap everywhere. Mounds of garbage. I'm talking *mountains* of actual trash. Like the city had run out of space at the landfill and decided to just dump it off in our living room. "What the *fuck!?*" Simon rages. He throws his suitcase against the wall and creates a three-foot-wide hole in the dry wall. "Dude, what are you doing?" I say, appalled at his sudden shift into unhinged insanity. "We're gonna have to pay for that, Simon!" I say, getting in his face. Simon lifts a fist up at me, and I back down. Holy shit. This kid is about to punch me. "Don't fucking come near me, Nick. I will break your face." The way he says it, the way he clenches his teeth together. The mania in his eyes. He's deadly serious. He's my friend, and he's about to knock me on my ass. Like, for real. Do friends treat each other like this? All these years, was I even his *friend*? I'm about to cry, but I'll be damned if Simon sees me cry, so I storm out of the room and up the stairs. I step over piles of magazines and plastic cups to make way into my new bedroom. I sit on the carpet, and I silently cry.

"Look, man, I'm sorry. It's not you," Simon says, standing in the doorway of my unfurnished room. "Let's clean this place up and make it our own." I forgive him instantly. I just want his acceptance. Sure, I'm still a little upset, but he's my hero. And it's easy to excuse your heroes of their bad behavior. We spend the next two hours getting drunk on port wine and picking up garbage left behind by the former tenants. This place is a hellhole. It should be absolutely 100 percent illegal to rent out a place in this condition. That pudgy little bastard with his shit-stained shirt, peddling property that the city forgot about. The place is sweltering hot. Thank God for the single box fan sitting in the window of the kitchen, blowing black mold and dust into our lungs. I am shirtless and glistening with sweat. Simon is drunkenly eating pizza, lying on the floor. He has spray-painted SAY LA VIE above the gaping hole that he made with his suitcase. The sun is setting, and I'm dizzy on cheap booze and eighteen-year-old stupidity. We smoke weed on the back porch and fall asleep in a heap of dirty laundry to a Neutral Milk Hotel record. My dream has come true, I guess. I'm living my life. I'm out in the big world. Say la vie.

 "Get up, asshole," someone says. Sounds like Simon. My eyes are crusted shut, and I'm exceptionally hungover. I rub the boogers from my eyeholes. "What?" I ask, squinting at the body standing over me. Yep, it's Simon. "You stole my shoes, you dick. Get up and find my shoes." Simon is in an exquisitely bad mood this morning. "I'm late for work. Let's go." He takes a hit of his Pall Mall and pulls a vibrating phone out of his pocket. "I can't talk. I'm late for work, Mom. I love you too. But I'm late." He hangs up. "Dude, I didn't steal your shoes. They're in the microwave." I point to the kitchen. "You put your shoes in the microwave and cried about your grandma last night." He walks over to the microwave and opens it up. "Sorry," he mumbles, grabbing his microwaved shoes. A rare apology. I savor it. The front door slams shut, and I'm alone. There he goes. Off to his "job" as a chicken sexer. I swear to God, the kid works at a poultry factory thirty minutes outside of the city, inspecting chicken genitals for eight hours a day. I can only imagine how pissed off he looks while he listens to indie rock on his iPod and shaves off a few feathers to see if the chicken has a vagina or a penis.

The solitude is maddening. A baby bird chirps outside my window. A dog barks next door. A fly makes an unfortunate layover into the window fan and gets spit up all over the wall. Fly organ casserole. I put on a clean shirt, or rather a shirt that doesn't smell *that* bad, and I make my way into the kitchen for a smoke and a morning beer. That's all I do in here. Drink and smoke. Smoke and drink. My mom would put her foot up my ass if she could see me now. My phone rings. It's the ringer that comes with the phone when  you buy it. An obnoxiously upbeat nightmare of bleeps and bloops. I throw the cigarette into the toilet and piss it out. "Nicky, it's Dad. We haven't heard from you in a whole day. Is everything cool?" my poor dad asks. "Dad, I'm fine. Leave me alone." I hang up, pissed off that he doesn't trust me. Pissed that he even bothered me out of the blue. I'm an adult. This is my new home. And my dad is treating me like a fetus. The phone rings again. This time it's my mother. Uh-oh. "You hung up on your father? Who do you think you are? Give me that envelope back with all the money I gave you to live on." My mom is no bullshit. She knows that I'm not some freeloader punk. She knows this is a moment in my life and nothing more. "You want me to cook you dinner and have Daddy drop it off?" I hesitate. "Sure."

That night, my dad drops off my mother's famous lasagna (modified to be vegan) and gets a load of our lair of filth and depravity for the first time. "You *live* in this?!" he explodes. "Nick, this is disgusting. You can't live like this. You need to buy some furniture and clean this crap up. I can't believe this. Jesus, Nick!" My dad is flipping out. His face is beet red. He looks at me like I'm a stranger. It's the saddest look you've ever seen.

"YOU'RE BETTER THAN THIS. YOU'RE ACTING LIKE A LOSER!"

The word hits me like a torpedo. That awful word. The L-word. *Loser.* And coming from my old man's mouth, it hurts even worse. He's my real hero. He's my *dad*. He raised me to be a decent human being. And right now, I'm the opposite of that. I have a serious attitude problem. I'm a glorified douchebag. My clothes smell like weed and vegan cheese. I listen to horrible music because it's cool. I wear sunglasses *indoors*, for Christ's sake. I'm a piece of crap. And my dad is right. My focus is gone, my future is dim, and I'm a waste of space. I'm going through a goddamn phase. And it has to end now.

The next morning, Simon is smoking a bong in the lotus position next to a topless sleeping brunette. His shaggy hair and unkempt beard don't look attractive today. His eyes are glazed over, his expression stoned and vacant. He looks like a homeless pirate. "What the fuck is up, sleepyhead?" Simon asks, coughing smoke into the air. "I'm going out to get a job. I need to find a job and make some money. I can't sleep all day and smoke weed with you anymore." Simon says nothing. The girl sits up and doesn't open her eyes. She just yawns and says, "Let's have sex." "No, baby. Sammy is moving in, and I have to help. I'm sorry, baby." Baby, baby, baby. If only he treated me as nicely as he treats this girl he met at a bar twelve hours ago. "Who's Sammy, Simon?" I ask. I've never even heard of a Sammy before, so this is news to me. "Someone else is moving into our house?" I can feel the shift. It's like the earth has cracked under the house and we're drifting apart. Two land masses splitting off into the sea. I don't see him as a bohemian god today. I see him as a chicken sexer. "Chill, homie. Sammy is my boy. He's gonna write poetry with us. He's the best poet in Cleveland," Simon boasts.

I don't even care who Sammy is. I don't care if he's Sammy Davis Jr. incarnate. I don't want anything to do with this person. A poet? Come on! Who's a poet anymore? Didn't Ginsberg say everything there was to be said? I grab Simon's bong out of the center of the room, and before he can do anything, I am bursting through the front door and onto the lawn. I lay it on its side, and smoke pours out into the dewy grass. I grab a rock from the garden and smash it with all my strength.

Goodbye, bong. Hello, black eye.

Simon comes storming out of the house and leaps off the porch with his fist extended and lands a fat punch to my face.

I spend the night with an ice pack over my left eye, smoking joints and watching *The Simpsons* with Simon and his dumb new girlfriend (whose name is literally Analanna—a combination of the words *anal* and *Anna*. Swear to Christ). We are friends again, I guess. The roller coaster of friendship. The gray areas of human connection. Why do we fall in and out of love? Why is it so hard to hate someone who makes you so goddamn angry? "I'm a dick. I didn't mean to smash your bong," I say. "Oh, really? It was an *accident*? Dude, you threw a fucking rock at it." A knock at the door. Simon gets up slowly and coolly walks over to see who it is. "What's up?" a voice says from the other side. It's Sammy. Simon opens the door to reveal the new addition to the skinny hippie club, a local poet named Sammy. His real name is Paul, but according to Simon, "He took on the name Sammy when he became a poet." What a crock of shit. "Hey, bro. I'm Sammy. I'm the future of modern American poetry," he says, flashing a peace sign and a crooked smile. This bozo is dead serious, and I'm doing my best not to laugh in his face. I mean, come on. Who says that kind of stuff when you first meet someone? Who says that stuff *period*?

Sammy paces around our living room, spouting off anti-American, capitalism-hating poems that make me want to throw up. Look, I'm as punk rock as the next guy, but this kid is so far up his own ass, he can taste his breakfast from last week.

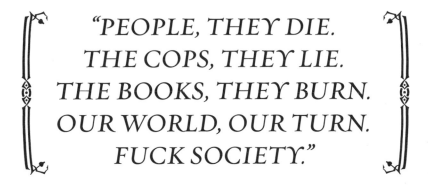

"PEOPLE, THEY DIE. THE COPS, THEY LIE. THE BOOKS, THEY BURN. OUR WORLD, OUR TURN. FUCK SOCIETY."

Sammy sits down against the wall with his head in his lap, faking some sort of emotional exhaustion from "speaking the truth" or some shit. He's such a poser, I can't even bear to be in the same room. "Okay, guys. I gotta go. I'm meeting my girlfriend for tacos." Sammy doesn't even look up from his crotch, he just sits there in a ball and sulks like the misunderstood poet that he is. Simon waves me off and leans in to kiss his dumb girlfriend. "Do you guys want anything?" The girl, between smooches, gets out the words "cheese" and "quesadilla," but Sammy manages to come out of his artistic stupor to say, "Cheese is the by-product of mechanized animal abuse and factory-farm evil." "Forget it," I say, defeated. These people are something else.

"This is Brutus. He bites really hard, so just don't get near his mouth or look him in the eyes," says the big girl who's standing in my kitchen. She's a friend of Simon's, apparently. A lesbian from Canton. I don't know her name, and she's now living in our house. Sleeping on the floor of our living room. She's covered in bad tattoos and petting a mangy pit bull who's balls are squashed against our tile floor. The words *FUCK* and *SHIT* are scrawled across the knuckles of her left and right hands, respectively. The *SHIT* hand is rubbing her dog. The lesbian's eyebrows are shaved off. She picks up one of the apples I bought with money from my mom's envelope and takes a bite out of it. I chomp down on my lip so I don't say something that I'll immediately regret.

Sammy enters the kitchen from the backdoor and wipes his greasy hands on the countertop. "You guys are out of paper towels again," he says, looking directly at me as if it's *my* problem.

"Why don't you buy some, Sammy? We all need to wipe. Or actually, can you write a poem about it? Write us a paper towel poem," I say, staring into his soul. I hope he can feel how angry I am. I hope he can *taste* it.

Simon glides into the room. I've never been this angry before. "Hey, Simon. Why don't you put on some clothes for a minute and go buy us some paper towels? Your buddy Sammy here needs to wipe his greasy hands. And your friend with the dog, she's eating my fruit. So, can you go out and buy us some more fruit?" Simon ignores me and heads straight for the shitter. He doesn't even close the door. He just opens his bathrobe and takes a nasty dump right there in front of everyone. We can hear it drop into the toilet like a bomb. He's in a daze. He doesn't even notice us watching him. His penis lies over the filthy toilet seat like a sleeping slug. His wiry pubes look like a beard. His penis looks like a Muppet's nose. I'm sick to my stomach. The smell of his dump gets the dog riled up, so it starts barking while the lesbian holds him back. "Come on, Brutus. Chill. Chill, Brutus," she says, while eating the apple that my mom paid for. Sammy pushes the bathroom door closed with his foot.

The dog keeps barking. His huge dog balls keep bouncing. The lesbian is still chomping on my apple. It's all too much. I have to get the fuck out of here right now. Just when I'm about to leave the house, three thumps on the front door. The hand of the law. I just feel it. That's not some kid looking to squat. That's not another deranged friend of Simon's. It's a cop. I feel it in my bones. I feel it in my butthole. The walls are covered in graffiti. There are spent joints crushed into the carpet. Mangled beer cans are littered all up and down the staircase, and they smell like skunk farts. This cop is here to arrest us, and I'm not ready to go to jail. Simon walks past me in a bathrobe, followed by Sammy, followed by the lesbian and her dog, followed by a blonde girl in a jean skirt who I've never seen before, and he opens the door. Simon looks high out of his gourd, and I'm sure he is. I cringe as the door swings open. It's not a cop, though. It's our landlord. Pudgy. And Jesus H. Christ, he's *pissed*.

"What in God's name is going on in here?" he asks, pushing his way into the house. He's maybe four-foot-eleven, but he's got a new attitude that adds an extra foot or two. "Who the *hell* are all these people?" he yelps. Brutus, the big-balled pit bull is showing Pudgy his fangs. "I'm Darlene. I'm a friend of Simon's. I'm gonna have to ask you to keep your voice down," the lesbian requests, but Pudgy isn't having it. He's heated up. Sweat drips down his forehead. His cheeks are red with fury. "You signed a lease, boys! You signed a goddamn lease! You can't have *all* these people living here. Darlene and you, and you, and this dog, all of you have to get the hell out of here right now!" Pudgy loses it. When I met him, he looked like he couldn't hurt a fly. But today, he looks like his toupee could catch fire at any moment. He looks like a hornet. Like a fat little landlord hornet who will sting the shit out of somebody. "Sir, you have to back down right now," Darlene demands in her deep voice.

I look at the dog, and he's ready to eat this guy's face off. She is holding him back for now, but one slip of her finger and Brutus will make a lunch out of Pudgy's piggy cheeks.

"You have two hours," Pudgy says, lowering his voice to a human level, "to pack your stuff. And get out of here. All of you."

Pudgy leaves, slamming the door shut, barely avoiding an attack from the most hard-core dog in Cleveland. Sammy is unmoved. He's humming something under his breath. "Sammy, what the fuck?" I say. "Get your shit and get out of here, man. Come on." Sammy looks at me, laughs a little laugh, and puts his arms on both of my shoulders. He penetrates into the core of my eyes. Fuck that, he stares into my *soul*. And he says, "This is an illusion."

With that, he's gone. He packs up the few shirts he owns and his little poetry notebook, and he's out of there. Darlene takes a few of my mom's apples for the road and leaves out the backdoor. I watch them leave. Her dog's gigantic testicles bungee up and down, hypnotizing me. I snap out of it and look for Simon. "Dude, Simon. Come on, man. We gotta get the hell out of here. I'm moving back home."

The anonymous blonde is already in the grass out back, rolling around like an idiot. I watch through the kitchen windows. She didn't have any bags to pack. Hell, she isn't even wearing underwear. I can see Simon in his bathrobe, telling her to get up and leave, but she just laughs at him like a child and pulls him down into the grass. They lie there together, and she lights him a cigarette as I bag up my belongings at 120 Random. Godspeed, you filthy hellhole. I will absolutely, positively, 100 percent not miss you.

 Simon is eating ramen noodles out of a saucepan that my mom bought for me. The house is empty except for two chairs, a saucepan, two forks, and a pack of Pall Mall cigarettes. We're sharing a bowl of soup together. Our only sober meal of the entire five days. Our Last Meal. Our landlord thinks the house is vacant. "So we only made it a week. Wow," Simon says, staring into his ramen. "Yep," I say, kind of laughing a bit. "It's ridiculous, Simon. We were great friends in high school. We made art together. Music together. We went to the park every day after school and smoked cigarettes and listened to CDs in your car. You were my best friend. I just . . . I guess I just don't know. I don't know what happened." Simon slurps the remaining noodles up. "Dude, we are just different people. You tried to be me. And you should be you. And I'm proud that you're your own dude. So, just be you," he says, finally looking up at me. I want to cry, but I shouldn't. I don't want him to see me cry. I'm too cool for that, remember?

The moldy, hot June air sits stagnant in the living room of 120 Random Road. Simon gets up from his plastic Ikea chair, and I get up from mine. He sets down the saucepan and buries his face into my shoulder. There isn't even time to think. He just stands there. And he hugs me. And I hug him back. Hard. And we don't say a word. We just hug. And he knows that I know that we will always have this memory. And fuck the future. Who cares about that? We were friends, and we will be friends, even when we aren't.

My dad picks me up at 4:00 in the afternoon. "So, Nick. You made it one business week. You ready to come home now?" my dad asks, and I cry. I cry so hard. Like a baby. I thought I could be a man. I thought I could live on my own. I had this crazy idea that I was independent. That I was an adult. That the number eighteen meant I was finally free. But family is the most important thing there is. Friends will come and go. But your tribe is your tribe. And they will be there when you come back through that door with your head down and your dreams crushed, and they will hold you while you cry. They will say, "I told you so," but that's okay, because family is about honesty. And you don't have to be something you're not. You can just be yourself. And they will love you forever and ever and ever.

"Mom's making meatloaf tonight," my dad says.

I wipe my tears and laugh as we glide along the
old Cleveland highway.

"I guess I'm not a vegan anymore."